# A THIRST
# FOR WHOLENESS

*While this book is designed for the reader's personal enjoyment and profit, it is also intended for group study. A Leader's Guide with Victor Multiuse Transparency Masters is available from your local bookstore or from the publisher.*

# A·THIRST·FOR WHOLENESS

## Jay E. Adams

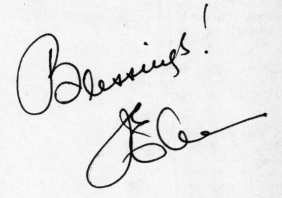

# VICTOR BOOKS®
A DIVISION OF SCRIPTURE PRESS PUBLICATIONS INC.
USA CANADA ENGLAND

*Recommended Dewey
Decimal Classification: 248.4
Suggested Subject Heading:*
SPIRITUAL LIFE

*Library of Congress Catalog
Card Number: 87-62608
ISBN: 0-89693-455-1*

# CONTENTS

# FOREWORD

For generations, psychologists and psychiatrists, peeping into what some of them choose to call the human "psyche," have been trying to understand the inner life of human beings. Thousands, engaged in this endeavor, on all continents, have written millions of pages about it, and yet the results have been utterly disappointing. Ideas about human inner life have only proliferated rather than converged in the kind of deepening consensus that is found in other disciplines. So serious is this failure to attain a consensus that it may fairly be said that among psychotherapists confusion reigns. One psychologist, recently commenting on this phenomenon, wrote that it constitutes nothing less than "a babble of voices."[1] Another, more euphemistically calls the confusion "a ballet of differences."[2] Joseph Carey reports, "Health officials point out that it is difficult to assess the effectiveness of the 250 different psychotherapies now in use."[3]

Two hundred-fifty psychotherapies are now in use. Think of it! That means 250 differing views of human life, the nature and origin of human problems, and what to do about them.

Think what it would mean if there were 250 differing views of any other discipline—electricity, air traffic control, shipbuilding, or whatever. Chaos!

It is time to turn from unprofitable guesswork to hear what God has said about the matter. After all, He is the One who made you and knows all about you. I know of no better way to do so than by thoroughly studying the inner life of the human being in the Book of James.

I do not propose to psychologize Scripture. To do any such thing amounts to interpreting the Bible through the grid of one or more of the 250 man-made systems of psychology into which the Scriptures are then force-fitted. Instead, I propose to help you investigate what God *Himself* has said about the inner dynamics of your life. I plan, therefore, not to bring some external system or even a series of contemporary questions to the epistle, but simply to allow James himself to be our guide, leading us wherever he will.

You probably recognize the practical nature of what James has written, especially his emphasis on works as the fruit of genuine faith. That's good—but do you often find it difficult to follow his instructions? Many Christians do. One reason why is the failure to understand his insights into human dynamics.

James' basic concern is to help you become a *teleios* ("complete") person (James 1:4; 3:2; see also 1:17, 27). To do so, James not only encourages proper behavior, but also explains the inner dynamics that produce it. To be *complete* you must take these inner dynamics into account.

Many people have failed in the pursuit of holiness, in part, because, knowing what God requires, they did not know what they were up against when attempting to meet these requirements. And so they find themselves unable to make sufficient progress. You do not have to remain among that number.

James' method for helping you grow is unique. He alone provides *detailed* revelation from God about many of the forces at work within you. When you become aware of this emphasis, passages about the inner life jump out as you read. And yet, so far as I can tell, the territory is virtually unexplored. I propose, then, an expedition to locate and examine the primary places where God tells you about your inner life.

As you read, you will see how James' unrecognized emphasis was a major concern for him and is not merely a construct that I have imposed upon the book. It was while teaching a course entitled, "Counseling and the Book of James," that I began to recognize something of what James was up to. His insistent concern to explain the inner dynamics of human life kept intruding itself upon what I was teaching. As a result, I was forced to consider the matter subsequently—a study that fully confirmed my suppositions about his underlying purposes and method.

The book that you hold in your hand is the fruit of such further reflection. It is not a commentary. It does not deal with the whole Book of James. It is not a book on "James and counseling." Rather, this volume is an intensive study of what God has revealed through James about *you*, the *inner* you. My sole interest is to consider those outcroppings of divinely-revealed insights into your nature that keep popping up here and there throughout the book.

Obviously, James doesn't tell you *everything* you'd like to know about the dynamics of human life, nor even all that God wants you to know. There is more elsewhere in Scripture. James' uniqueness among New Testament writers lies not in the fact that he supplies insight into human dynamics, but that he makes such a point of doing so. He wants you to know that to become a "complete" Christian, you must understand the inner dynamics involved. James' emphasis, unique among New Testament books, plainly marks his letter as a piece of wisdom literature.

James' wisdom, while not providing a comprehensive treatise on all the inner workings of the human being, does supply basic insights needed to counter baneful patterns adopted by your sinful nature. Like all others, you have learned to use your inner capacities for sinful ends—even though God originally designed those capacities to facilitate holy living. James exposes those patterns, showing how they defeat you in your purpose to serve Christ. By laying before you exactly what you are up against, he wants to equip you to counter, avoid, and replace those patterns with biblical ones.

Many Christians have difficulty making spiritual progress. Perhaps you do. One of the causes for discouragement and defeat is a failure to understand and apply divine insights. My prayer is that by bringing these to light, you will find solid help in becoming God's *complete* Christian.

[1]John Leo, "A Therapist in Every Corner," *Time*, December 23, 1985, p. 59, at the Evolution of Psychotherapy Conference, Phoenix.
[2]John Leo, *op. cit.*
[3]"Dark Days for Psychiatry: A Search for Answers," *U.S. News and World Report*, Feb. 25, 1985, p. 74.

# YOU CAN BE A COMPLETE CHRISTIAN

"What's wrong with me? I never seem to get it all together. I think I'm growing spiritually in one area only to discover others in which I haven't even begun to make progress. I was making progress in my prayer life when here I go and blow it—letting my temper get the better of me. Is there no way to get a handle on the Christian life?"

That's what Fred, an exasperated husband, asked after he had blown up at his wife, saying all sorts of things he really didn't mean and had determined never to say again. The Book of James has the solution to Fred's dilemma. James will tell Fred how to deal with his anger and, in particular, how to "get it all together."

The object of James' book is to teach you to solve problems God's way so that you will become a mature Christian. James calls the mature Christian—who is in the process of resisting and overthrowing sin, whose faith is strong and unwavering, whose prayers are effective, and who knows how to endure trial—a "complete" (*teleios*) person.

Just what does that mean? The Greek word *teleios* is used in the expression "complete (*teleios*) and entire" (James 1:4). James' concern is the same as Fred's: getting it all together.

The word *teleios* is full of meaning, including the ideas of entirety, completeness, maturity, and even perfection. The last two concepts (maturity and perfection), however, are viewed from the perspective of *completeness*, the fundamental element in the term. Even today in the Greek language this element persists. For instance, in modern Greek, a *teleia* is a period, or complete stop, the mark used at the end of a sentence to indicate that the sentence is *complete*. Similarly, a "mature" person is one who has *completed* the maturation process that extends from childhood to adult life. According to James, a "perfect" person lacks nothing (v. 4); he is entire, complete. Biblically speaking, a *perfect person*, therefore, is one who *on all fronts* (without exception) is progressing in his Christian life—not one who no longer sins. In every area of his life, the process of maturation is properly at work.

James stressed this notion of completeness by using the phrase "complete and entire" (v. 4). The second word in the couplet, *holokleros,* refers to something with "every part intact," that "has all its parts," something with integrity. Both words are coupled together again in the same way in Colossians 4:12, indicating that the phrase "complete and entire" was commonly used to emphasize completeness.

We know James had completeness in mind not only because he used the common phrase for it, but because immediately afterward he explained that the *teleios* Christian "lacks nothing." One who lacks nothing, has everything; he is complete. James wants you to recognize possible lacks in your life and has written both to identify them and to tell you what to do about them.

This idea of completeness in James, whose writing in other respects closely approximates Old Testament wisdom literature, is probably borrowed from the Hebrew notion of the *tam* ("whole") person[1] found in Job 1:1, where Job is declared to be a "perfect" person. Job was not sinless, but he was a man of integrity. His life, *as a whole*, pleased God. Likewise, David expressed a determination to walk with integrity before his household (Ps. 101:2).

David, Job, and James were all talking about the same thing—a spiritually mature person who is moving ahead well in every area of life. This person is not sinless, nor has he reached some kind of perfection at which he can halt his forward progress in any of these areas. Rather, *without exception*, the complete person is making progress in all areas. That is James' concern. He wants you to become a well-rounded, complete Christian who lacks nothing. Are there areas in your life where gaps occur? Are there inner forces that win out over your better intentions? Then this book is for you.

God's concern for completeness clearly appears in James' exhortation, "Let endurance have its full (*teleion*) effect" or "complete work" (James 1:4). He is afraid some people will follow unwarranted means to avert trials, thus cutting short the maturation process that is tied into them. Apart from the good effects of endurance under trial, a Christian is incomplete. Endurance under trial has an inner "work" to do. That is why James encourages you to avoid shortcuts. He wants trials to produce endurance, which is part of God's "perfect [complete and completing] work."

What James teaches about testing and endurance is applicable to all that follows in his book. Such inner "works" or processes (e.g., "testing *works* endurance; endurance has its *work*," etc.) bring about completeness. By such means God's Spirit works to complete you. That is the first inner dynamic that James discusses—a positive one. It is essential to know

[1]The Hebrew word *tam* is frequently rendered *teleios* in the Septuagint (the Greek translation of the old Testament that was in common use in James' day).

about it so that you won't thwart its completing, integrating function.

But there are other dynamics at work—negative ones—of which you must be aware. Negative processes, when allowed to progress unchecked, have the opposite effect: they *dis*integrate life. James tells us, for instance, that double-mindedness (or doubting God's Word) destroys stability in every area of life; he mentions particularly how it debilitates prayer life. The Book of James helps you to recognize these positive and negative inner processes so that you will be able to encourage the former and counter the latter.

James warns that the destructive, sinful processes at work within you impede and undo the work of constructive, completing ones. These inner forces divide you and make you inconsistent, undependable, and immature. They tear large holes in the fabric of your spiritual life. By making you aware of these processes—just how they work, what their effects are, and how to identify them—James makes it possible to forestall them early on. Temptation, for instance, need not have *its* full effect. By appropriate action, it may be inhibited at any one of three transition points identified by James. In its stead the opposite process of building endurance may be initiated. Thus, the process which would potentially lead to sin, instead, may be replaced by a positive process that will produce spiritual growth.

So, there is something fresh in the Book of James that you must grasp to lead the productive, fruitful Christian life of a mature Christian. With this in mind, let's turn now to a detailed study of the specific processes delineated by James.

# YOU CAN FACE TRIALS WITH JOY

Bob was down in the dumps again. Barbara and the kids knew it the minute he opened the door. Things didn't go well at work. Not only did Bob's boss fail to congratulate him for the fine work he did on the last project—completing the job a week and a half before schedule—but, feeling rotten, the boss had found "reasons" to chew out everyone in the office, Bob included.

"The way they treat you down there when you do a good job," Bob growled, "makes you want to quit. Or . . . just put in time instead of giving it all you've got!"

"You didn't quit, did you?" asked Barbara.

"No, but I have half a mind to do so Monday."

"But, remember, Bob, you're not only working for your boss, 'It's the Lord Christ you serve'" (Col. 3:24).

"I know that, Barb. And as a Christian I know I shouldn't let it get me down. But, somehow or other, I just do."

Bob's struggle is not unusual. You too may have a similar problem. Only, maybe you'd like to go on strike as a wife or mother instead! Is there really a way to handle trials and troubles with joy instead of gloom, anger, or despair?

No one lives for very long in this world of sin without falling into trials. If you are not in the middle of one right now, chances are you have just emerged from one—perhaps not entirely unscathed.

As you consider the way you handle trials and troubles, perhaps you think, *Yeah, I'm pretty much like Bob.* Perhaps you get angry or go all to pieces. Whatever your response, it usually isn't joyful. And you know you certainly haven't learned to look at trials with the *unmixed* joy about which James writes.


## God's Analysis

James provides insight into the sinister forces that drag you down and cause you to respond wrongly to trouble. But he also sets before you the proper Christian response.

> My brothers, consider it entirely a happy situation
> when you fall into trials of various sorts (James 1:2).

James wants you to know that the complete Christian rejoices in trial because he considers it "entirely a happy situation" (literally, "all joy").

Notice James doesn't mention the complete Christian's outward response. What he describes is the inner response of the *teleios* person who "considers" the trial an unmixed joy. *That's* the difference between the mature Christian's response and Bob's. The mature Christian sees something in the trial that the immature Christian misses. If you could learn to view trials as he does, that would change a lot of things in your life, wouldn't it?

"Sure it would," you say, "but that's hard to do. I don't know how to control my feelings that way, so I go into a blue funk like Bob, or get angry or bitter. I don't see how I could ever learn to rejoice over trials."

The problem is that your feelings are headed in the wrong direction. That's because the sinful response pattern to trouble you have developed triggers all the wrong emotional responses. But God doesn't command you to feel joyful in trials. He knows you too well. You aren't constructed that way—you can't turn your feelings on and off like hot and cold water from a faucet. Emotions aren't under your direct control.

Look at verse 2 again. James doesn't say "feel joyful," about the trial, but *"consider* it all joy." Now, there's something you can do whether you feel like it or not. Indeed, this is not just good advice, but something you *must* learn to do; James lays it down as a command.

The word *consider* is the key to handling both inner and outer responses to trials (the right outer responses depend ultimately on the right inner ones). The word expresses what you must learn to do inside. It has to do with your thought processes. Bob, you, and others who handle trials poorly do so because of poor inner responses to them. Trouble comes, and you get angry, gloomy, or whatever, just as you have *learned* to. In fact, you taught yourself those responses so well that you automatically respond that way.

Now, consider a moment what has been going on inside Bob. His boss fails to compliment him for the job done well and, instead, chews him out. You can read Bob's thoughts by what he says to Barbara. He is disappointed. He tells himself, *This isn't fair. I deserve something better than that!* But no sooner does he begin to think that way than gloom begins to settle down on him like a dense fog. The more he allows himself to think like that, the gloomier he becomes and the worse things get.

"Yes, you say, that's exactly what happens. But I still claim I can't control my feelings."

Right! But you can control your thinking. It's what Bob *considers* the trial to be that controls his feelings. And that is explicitly where God tells you to focus your attention: on your thoughts, *not* on your feelings. Learn to *consider* the trial a ground for rejoicing. Don't allow the slightest negative thought about it to enter your mind. See this as God's world, under His sovereign control and *everything* that happens as a means of honoring Him and bringing good to His children.

Notice the word *consider* a bit more closely. It is a most revealing term that, in its primary usage, means not "consider," but "lead." Its secondary usage "consider, count, regard," comes from the idea of "leading one's self to think" one way or another, a fact that is altogether important to an understanding of James' command.[1]

In trials you cannot directly control your emotions, but you can change them indirectly by *leading* your mind toward the right biblical considerations. Thinking about trials God's way generates proper inner and outer responses. As you begin to see trials more and more from God's viewpoint, eventually you will reach the place where you too can rejoice in them.

This doesn't just happen; it takes a deliberate act to wrench your mind out of the pagan cesspool of thought into which you have allowed it to wade. Over the years, perhaps you have slackened the reins and allowed your mind to muck around in the swamps along the well-worn pathways of sin and misery— paths into which your sinful nature used to lead your mind. But now, redeemed by the blood of Christ, regenerated by His Spirit and given a new heart oriented toward God and capable of living for Him, you are able to seize control of the reins and lead your mind to the pure, refreshing waters of life.

In other words, in any and all trials, if you deliberately take the time and make a prayerful effort to consider them as God

[1]That the primary meaning was never lost in favor of the secondary one seems certain since, in modern Greek, the secondary meaning used by James disappeared while the primary notion of leading remained. Thus, in James' time, the nuance of *leading* one's thoughts was always present.

does (Isa. 55:7-9), you will reach the place where you look on them entirely as a blessing—and rejoice. But you will not rejoice until you learn to *consider* trials what God sees them to be.

Even then, of course, that does not mean you should rejoice over pain, injustice, and other miseries. It does not mean that you will wear a silly grin and tell everybody, "Praise the Lord, anyway." It does not mean that you never shed a tear again or feel the pains of sorrow or loss. No, James is saying none of these things.

James can write as he does because he knows that joy is deeper than happiness. Unlike happiness, which is based on circumstances, joy is based on God's promises. That makes it possible to rejoice in the midst of trial, and even in pain (see Acts 5:40-41), not as a masochist who wants to suffer, but as a Christian who sees more in the trial than the trial itself—who sees beyond it to the joyful outcome (Heb. 12:2).

When you consider biblically what the trial is all about and see it the way God does—as a means of making you complete—you can "count it all joy" and rejoice! The Christian, unlike the humanist, knows that God is in the trial, at work, accomplishing all His purposes. That turns otherwise meaningless, absurd circumstances into joyful events.

Many Christians wonder why God doesn't take a more direct hand in their lives. Well, He does! They simply fail to *consider* what He is up to. God is at work chiseling away the rough edges, conforming you to the image of Christ, sanctifying, completing you—in trials! Thus, trials, upon proper reflection by the Christian, become a ground for joy rather than gloom. They are evidence that God is at work in your life, making you the *teleios* person He wants you to be.

You will never be able to handle trials until you have exchanged your own erroneous view of trouble for God's holy, correct view. God looks toward the outcome, what the trial is designed to do. Viewed that way, like Jesus, you too can "endure" trials "for the joy set before" you. Jesus considered the cross an entirely joyful event, despite His agony and suffering, because His eyes were set on that which it would accomplish (Heb. 12:2). This inner dynamic worked for Jesus, and it will work for you.

According to James, the same dynamic will work in "all sorts of trials" (James 1:2). The word translated "various sorts" literally means "many colored, variegated." The power of this inner dynamic is not restricted to a certain class of trials. God, the Master Painter, works in the entire spectrum of problems through which you pass in life. He is busy making you into a new person by the fiery reds of affliction, the icy blues of sorrow, the murky browns of failure, and the sickly yellows of illness and disease. God is at work; on His palette is every hue and intensity of the rainbow.

## Your Problem

Well, that is God's analysis of the situation: you can rejoice over trials when you recognize them for what they are—the evidence of God's hand at work, shaping you into the *teleios* person He wishes you to become. It is possible for you to do so because God never commands His children to do anything that He is unwilling to give them both the wisdom and the strength to do—if they are only willing.

Commentators sometimes have difficulty understanding why James seems to begin his letter somewhat abruptly. James, the leading pastor of the congregation of Jerusalem, knew people. God gave him insight into people's inner reasonings, doubts, and fears. James knew that those caught in sin, those with broken hearts, those struggling with temptation, confusion, and doubts want help—and they want it right away. And he knew they needed some straight talk.

When you go to the dentist you don't want him to talk about all sorts of unrelated matters. You tell him, "Here's where it hurts—bad!" You want relief and you want it in a hurry! There is time for small talk later. James is like a good dentist; quite abruptly he says, "Consider it an entirely happy situation when you fall into trials of various sorts." James gets right to the point.

But what he says isn't what many of the Jerusalem Christians wanted to hear. They expected sympathy. They wanted him to commiserate. Indeed, at first what James says seems cruel. Think of it! In the midst of all sorts of trials he lays a new responsibility on them: count trials a joy. Unthinking people, who do not consider life from a biblical perspective, don't want to be told that they should count their troubles a joy. Perhaps you too think like that.

Consider once more our friend the dentist. He looks at the aching tooth and he says, "I'm afraid it'll have to come out." Again, no sympathy! He just tells you that in the midst of your suffering you will have to undergo even more pain. But you submit to the pain he inflicts because you can see relief beyond the needle, the pliers, and the pain.

James isn't cruel. The Spirit of God led Him to write, "You've got problems? Then consider how to be happy." That's a kindness. As James says, however, it takes *consideration* to see this. James wants to awaken you *from the outset* to the importance of the right attitude toward all the problems he will write about in his letter. He wants to sweep aside self-pity, discouragement, anger, or anything else that would keep you from considering reality for what it is. The only way that will happen is for you to begin with the proper, godly perspective on trouble—no matter how it hurts.

Moreover, James knows what every good surgeon knows: your inner attitude is all important. If you go into surgery talking about your will and what kind of flowers you want on your casket, your surgeon will be concerned. People die from wrong attitudes. Likewise, people with positive attitudes tend to survive surgery and recover sooner. In the same way, your inner thinking must be positive in order for you to survive life's trials.

James begins his letter with this command in order to create an attitude that will be accepting of the teaching that follows. He will realize his desire to bring about your completeness only by providing the information, directions, insight, and motivation to lead your mind into the right attitudes. We shall look at these matters in the chapters that follow, but first consider one more fact about trial that James mentions: when trials are not prematurely cut short, they will produce endurance.

### Endurance

God uses trials to accomplish His purposes in our lives; trials have a good effect—when handled His way. One of those good effects is endurance. Here is a concrete result to consider when you think about counting trials an unmixed joy. Throughout the centuries, from the apostles onward, Christians have endured disgrace, loss, deprivation, torture, and even death for the sake of Christ. Some have gallantly faced lions, the stake, and every sort of hardship successfully, to the honor of their Lord. But other Christians failed, recanting, betraying, and denying Christ. What made the difference? Some had *endurance;* others did not.

Endurance is the ability to hang in there when the going gets tough. The complete Christian honors Christ when it is difficult to do so because he has developed endurance. In the critical hour, he does not cave in.

James tells us to consider trials a joy, "knowing that the testing of your faith works endurance. And let endurance have its full effect, that you may be complete and entire, lacking in nothing" (James 1:3-4). Faith is strengthened by handling trials God's way. Trials considered joyful because of their outcome, will produce the ability to endure—even to death. In the crucial hour, when they are called upon to stand for Christ, too many Christians crumble. They give up—on marriages, on friends, on children, on the church, on their testimony, on God!

That happens because in many smaller trials those Christians failed to grow. They handled the trials wrongly. When the time came to stand firm, they failed. If Bob continues to treat trials at work and elsewhere by spreading clouds of gloom, he will likely come apart when the crucial hour strikes.

God holds you responsible to endure. If you give up, saying, "It's too much" or "It's too tough" when God's Word says differently (1 Cor. 10:13)[2], you will remain spiritually immature. Instead of strengthening your faith by learning to handle trials God's way, you weaken your faith by repeated failures.

God is preparing you for the days to come. It is like preparing for the Olympics. For years, swimmers, runners, and other athletes work at building endurance in less than dramatic ways so that in competition they will have what it takes when every ounce of perseverance is called for. No one wins the great contest who has not won many seemingly insignificant ones first. A lot may hang on your daily performance in a trial: your family's welfare, a witness for Christ in a critical moment, the good of His church. Joseph didn't know what great issues he would face in the pit, in Potiphar's house, or in the prison, but he was faithful in all. As a result, when God put Joseph in a

[2]See my pamphlet on 1 Corinthians 10:13, *Christ and Your Problems.* Presbyterian and Reformed Pub. Co., Nutley, NJ: 1972. In this verse God says that the problems Christians face are not unique, are uniquely suited to each Christian, and will end. All of this, He reveals, "in order that you may be able to *endure* it."

place of real significance, he was ready for the test and did not fail. All along, he had the right attitude about his trials. He told his brothers, "You meant evil against me; but God meant it for good, to bring it about that many people should be kept alive as they are today" (Gen. 50:20, RSV).

## Your Danger

In every trial there is grave danger of falling into a trap. You will be tempted to cut short the process of building endurance. That happens whenever you do not "let endurance have its full effect." If God cuts the trial short, fine. If you cut it short by following God's directions, fine. But if in some unbiblical way you cut the process short, you will lack the spiritual endurance the trial was designed to produce. At the moment you need that spiritual strength, you will find yourself incomplete.

James warns about the danger of cutting the trial short in the wrong way. If it were not possible to do so, James wouldn't have included the warning. It is understandable for you to end your suffering as quickly as possible, but if you do so before the trial has done its job, you will only face another trial until the spiritual lesson is learned. That's what happened to Jonah. He unnecessarily heaped misery on top of misery by handling his trials his way. In the end, he had to go God's way anyhow. There was no shortcut.

How can a trial be cut short? The desire to relieve pain and suffering may be so great that you may be anxious for relief. You may turn to medicine, shock treatment, or whatever relief is available to lessen your pain when an organic problem is not the cause. You may give up, stop struggling, fall apart, or blow up before reaching the blessing. Many Christians are quitters. Or you may give into some temptation arising out of the trial. You may settle for less than God has planned for you. You may reach for solutions that weaken rather than strengthen your faith. And, you may circumvent the trial altogether by refusing to assume some responsibility that is rightfully yours.

The full effect of endurance changes you and strengthens you; it does not change your situation. And, most of all, through trial God is bringing you into a closer relationship to Himself. To cut short the effect of a trial is to reduce the godly discipline that you so need to become complete. The trial may be considered a joyful event when you see that God is at work completing you and making you a person who can endure because you know God better.

The psalmist understood these things and wrote, "Before I was afflicted I went astray; but now I keep Thy saying" (Ps. 119:67, MLB). Like James, he too saw that trials strengthen spiritual life. Affliction, rightly considered and handled, enabled the psalmist in a new way to follow God's law. He concluded, "It is good for me that I was afflicted, so that I may learn Thy statutes" (v. 71, MLB).

Why not determine to deliberately consider the trial you are facing an unmixed joy? If you do, it will make all the difference.

# THREE

# YOU CAN RESIST
# TEMPTATION

"I did it again! Here I had determined to resist the temptation, but as soon as it poked its ugly head up—I fell! I'll admit, at the moment it didn't look so ugly as it does now and I was taken in. What's wrong with me? Must I continue sinning and repenting over the same sin? Will I ever break out of this kiss-and-make-up syndrome with God? Why can't I ever seem to make progress? Is there any hope for me?"

That's what Phyllis asked when talking to her pastor about her problem of overspending. But it might as readily have been Mark, struggling to overthrow the temptation to view pornographic video tapes and movies on TV.

Perhaps in periods of self-disgust you've also said things like that. Possibly, even now as you read, you find yourself relating to Phyllis' words. Let me say at the outset: there is hope. James recognizes your problem, describes the forces of temptation at work within you, and tells you what can be done about them.

Let no one who is tempted say, "I am being tempted by God," because God isn't tempted by evil things and He tempts no one with them. Instead, each one is tempted by his own desires; like a fish going after bait he is hooked and pulled up. Then when desire has conceived it gives birth to sin, and sin, when fully matured, brings forth death. Don't be misled, dear brothers (James 1:13-16).

## Trials and Temptations

Because there is some confusion about the words *trial* and *temptation*, James distinguishes the two. God doesn't tempt His children, even though He does strengthen and complete them through trials. The distinction is interesting, especially in the original where the very same word is used for both.[1] Actually, this term takes its meaning from the context in which it is used. That, in itself, is instructive: the same experience may be viewed from either of two perspectives. Indeed, the whole point of James' teaching is that the same event can go either way; it can become a trial strengthening you or a temptation weakening you—depending on how you respond to it.

If Phyllis had successfully resisted the temptation to buy when she shouldn't and Mark had not watched pornographic material that he shouldn't, they would have grown. As it is, they did not grow; they were further weakened. What makes the event either a trial or a temptation for you is your response to it.

From God's perspective, the event is an opportunity, designed for your good; a trial that can strengthen. From Satan's perspective, the event has potential for evil that will weaken you. In every trial, you should remember the double possibili-

[1]The word switches its meaning from *trial* (vv. 2, 12) to *temptation* (vv. 13-14).

ty. Some Christians never gain the twofold perspective. They construe every event only as a temptation and miss the opportunity for inner growth. Seeing only temptation defeats and discourages and, in part, accounts for their failure to overcome. The first step, therefore, is to discover the full potential for good that exists in every event, even if at first the situation seems like a temptation. So-called positive thinkers see only the good side; the possibilities and the potentials in the trial. Because they do, it is possible for them to treat a trial too lightly, unaware of the dangers in it, and thus fall into one of the many traps Satan sets along the way. Failure to recognize both possibilities is dangerous.

Why does James bring up this subject? He had been discussing trials, and his desire to help Christians become complete. Temptation, yielded to, is a serious impediment to spiritual maturity. To grow and become more complete, it is necessary to learn about temptation so that you may successfully combat it.

### Who's to Blame?

Clearly, not every believer handles temptation well. James says, "If you sin during a time of trial, don't blame God. He sent it for your good; you misused it. You are to blame if you yield to temptation. God has no propensity to sin and He doesn't tempt you to commit sin. Every time of trouble comes as a wall with two doors; on the one is written *God's way to victory*, on the other *Satan's way to defeat*. The fact that you opened the wrong door and stepped in is not God's fault, but yours."

James explains, "The force at work within you when you turn trouble into temptation is not some foreign power that invaded you from without; it is your own desire. That is your principal problem." The problem is not in God; it is not in the event; it is in you. You turn the event into an occasion to satisfy some desire. The event may be innocent or sinful. But, if innocent, it becomes sinful if indulged at the wrong time, in the wrong way, or for the wrong purpose. The way James puts it is that you entice yourself to sin. By allowing the outside event to stir some inner desire, you create the temptation.

The flash of the lure you thought you saw moving through the water was really in your own eye. Jesus said, if your "eye is healthy" you will not see it. It is the "evil eye" that is not "single" that causes you to see darkness rather than light (Matt. 6:22-24). The person or thing became a lure when you considered it such. No beautiful woman can tempt you if your heart is right. Strong drink is no temptation when your inner desires are under control. You, not God, are to blame. James doesn't even bring Satan into the picture. You must take full responsibility for your sin. You can blame it on no one but yourself.

Blameshifting has been a problem ever since Eden. Adam blamed his wife and God Himself for his sin; Eve blamed the serpent. God held all three responsible—each for his own sin. Today husbands and wives still engage in the nefarious practice of blameshifting. Here, through James, God says, "*Each one* is tempted by *his own* desires" (1:14). It is a matter of individual responsibility in every instance. When you lust after another person, it is because of your own desires. Sin of the heart means allowing your desire rather than God's commandments to direct you.

## Knowledge Helps

"If I had only known. . . ." That's what you hear Christians saying after they have transgressed God's Word. Well, spoken seriously (not as an excuse), there's some truth in what they say. Knowledge *does* help. In fact, that is the second reason why God pulls aside the curtain and gives you a view of the dynamics at work within. He is concerned not only to place the responsibility where it belongs, but also to enlighten you. When you know what is going on, you can take steps to resist the dark forces within that turn trials into sin. Knowledge is important, but it is not everything. Without obedience, or as James puts it, without works, faith, no matter how well-informed, is dead.

**The Process**
As James describes it, the process involves either being "hooked and drawn up" or "enticed (drawn aside) and caught by bait." Translated either way, the passage pictures a fish enticed by the fisherman's lure. The sinning Christian is lured away from the place of safety by his own desire. And this desire, indulged, leads to transgression (v. 15). It should be your concern then to assume responsibility for temptation, learn the process by which you provoke it, and take measures to counter it.

The attraction of the fisherman's lure suggests another attraction to James. He mentions adultery. Moving from the metaphor of the fish, James describes the progress of sin in terms of a geneological line in which the grandchild of sinfully-indulged desire is death. That sin begets death is understandable because, from the beginning, sin carried death within. The harlot Desire entices in the same way a lure attracts fish. When you agree to sin with her in your imagination, your desire and your will inwardly consent to sin. That is sin in the heart. It is, in effect, infidelity toward God—finding an inner delight in doing something God forbids. Inner, sinful intercourse with a wrong desire, in time, leads to the conception and birth of the outer act of sin. Thus, unchecked desire in time, gives birth to transgressions. Finally, if this sin grows to maturity—i.e., if it becomes the continued practice of one's life; the sort of practice of sin that characterizes the life of an unbeliever who is never converted—its ultimate end is eternal death (Rom. 6:23). Hort puts it this way:

> The double image distinguishes the consent of the will (the man) to the desire from the resulting sinful act, which may follow either instantly or at a future time.[2]

God takes pains to describe this process of temptation from start to finish because it consists of a series of stages. And that means the process can be short-circuited. Just as you can miss the full blessings of a trial by illegitimately cutting short the trial that produces them, so too can you cut off the life cycle of sin at any step in the process.

Let's look briefly at each of the steps in order.

STEP ONE: INTERCOURSE (in the heart). An event occurs. Within, your desire stirs in response to it. You recognize this and *could* cut the process short before sinning in the heart by changing the direction of your thoughts (Phil. 4:8). You don't. Instead you allow your imagination to contemplate the possibility of sin. You assent to the sin in your mind; your mind goes to bed with the desire. You have sinned in your heart. That is what the writer of Proverbs was getting at when he warned against thinking about the adulteress' "beauty in your heart."

STEP TWO: CONCEPTION (in the heart). If this intercourse of the heart continues, conception of outer sin will occur. That is to say, next, you begin to contemplate actually carrying out the sin, not merely indulging in it in your heart.

---

[2]F.J.A. Hort, *James*, in *Expository and Exegetical Studies*. Klock and Klock Pubs., Minneapolis: 1980, p. 26.

Again, as you do this you can cut the process short by rejecting these plans, repenting of inner consent, and planning instead acts of outer righteousness.

STEP THREE: BIRTH (of sin; outer transgression). Sinful acts can be prevented by radical amputation (Matt. 5:28ff). You can guard against acts of sin (transgressions) through the radical amputation or elimination of whatever facilitates sin. That will lead to (1) awareness—it is impossible to sin automatically and unconsciously when you have eliminated those things that contribute to it; and to (2) a condition in which it is difficult to sin again in the same way. The latter requires putting impediments in the way.[3]

STEP FOUR: DEATH. It is interesting to think of death being "born!" Yet that is exactly the bold imagery that James uses. We need not concern ourselves with this matter since, for the Christian, death has been cut off by regeneration and justification. A true believer will not continue in the sin; he will repent (1 John 3:9-10). Thus, for the believer, the line leading to death has already been severed by Christ.

In summary, desire seizes upon an outer opportunity to assert herself, turning this event into a temptation. The two come together at desire's command and become the parents of transgression. In turn, in the unbeliever that temptation ultimately leads to the birth of spiritual death.

## Intercourse and Conception
Every Christian has the capacity to resist sin. And the best time to do so is before its conception in the heart. The heart is

[3]For a full discussion of the doctrine of radical amputation, see my book, *A Theology of Christian Counseling.* Zondervan Pub. House, Grand Rapids: 1979, chapter 16. Proverbs 5:8, 7:25 speak of the simple, but important and effective method of avoiding temptation (here, from the adulterous woman)—keeping out of her territory!

the inner life that you live before yourself and God alone. By understanding the alluring ways of your desires and refusing to consent to them, you will cut the sin process short before it has begun. But unless you recognize which temptations especially appeal to you, you will tend to deceive yourself. Remember James' last words on the subject: "Don't be misled." What are some of those ways you deceive yourself?

Prodded by teachings of self-love, TV commercials, and other forms of advertisement, desires within you urge "Go ahead; you deserve it!" You should keep in mind that you don't deserve anything, but that all good you have or ever will have is the gift of God. Remember, *deserve* is a concept that has only to do with condemnation, never with blessing. Christian, you *deserve* hell; you are going to heaven by the grace of God. Grace means that you are going to heaven *in spite of* what you *deserve*.

Desire may also try to allure you by telling you that you have a "need" for the forbidden pleasure. But according to Scripture, your needs are relatively few: "When we have food and clothing we shall be satisfied with these" (1 Tim. 6:8). In fact, if you boil it down to essentials, Jesus said, "There is need of but one thing"—the Word of Christ (Luke 10:42, MLB).

People used to say, "I need a fork to eat my food; I need a saw to cut the wood." They were speaking of relative needs; not compelling absolutes. This is a legitimate use of the word. And the need was for something external to themselves. Now, however, you hear people saying, "I have a need to do so and so." And they make these so-called internal needs sound like absolutes. If you need it, then by all means, you *must* have it, so it is not wrong to want it or get it. This humanistic philosophy holds that man is a creature of needs who must fulfill his needs or he cannot function well (as Christians construe it, "well" means obeying God). Hence, this new psychological construction—which now seems to be replacing the simple "I need a . . ." phrase—is used to justify all sorts of sin.

If you substitute the word *desire* for the word *need* whenever you run across the new construction, almost always you will come closer to the truth. Mark did not "have a need to view pornographic material"; he had a desire to. Phyllis didn't "have a need to overspend"; she wanted to. In both cases, when they gave in to their desires, they sinned. Contrary to James, the new construction excuses one from responsibility. When you think of desires as needs, it is harder to resist them. So, it is especially important in this day in which error about the inner functioning of the human being is so prevalent, to understand that what leads to sinful behavior is not inner needs but inner desires.

Many psychologists emphasize feelings, and taking their cue from them, stick slogans on their car bumpers reading, "If it feels good, do it." Those who follow that advice fall headlong into temptation. It is desire, always perceived as feelings, that James warns against. Not that desire *per se* is wrong, but it can *never* replace the Bible as a guide. Whenever the two conflict, desire must be rejected in favor of obedience to God's Word.

Jesus had no sinful desires. Temptation came only from without. We differ from Him at this point. But He did have desires. Like Him, you are tempted to fulfill even your good desires in wrong ways, at wrong times, for wrong purposes. Satan's ploy was to appeal to the fulfillment of right desires, wrongly (Matt. 4:1ff). Christ's temptations came from another, but they did appeal to His inner desires. Our temptations come both from within and from without. You, like Jesus, have one way of resisting temptation: by countering it with the appropriate Scripture which you must choose to obey rather than the desire. When tempted to look lustfully at another person, you must remind yourself, "You shall not commit adultery" (Ex. 20:14, RSV). "For to you the commandment is a lamp, the teaching a light, and the reproofs of discipline a way of life to keep you from the evil woman, from the smooth tongue of an unfamiliar woman" (Prov. 6:23-24, MLB). Here Scripture is clearly said to be the means for combating sexual temptation. When tempted to think revengefully, you should remember, "Vengeance is *Mine;* I will repay, says the Lord" (Rom. 12:19).

## Acts of Sin

The third stage in the steps of sin is its outward expression in words and deeds. Clearly, even if you sin in your heart it is not necessary for you to sin outwardly as well. Both the inner assent and the outer expression are sins and, before God, neither is worse than the other. Socially speaking, however, it is usually worse to sin outwardly as well. It is certainly better for another if you hate him in your heart, but do not follow through by shooting him in the head! Once you have committed inner sin, there is still the possibility of repenting of it and cutting off the process at this point. To go further and sin outwardly as well as inwardly only doubles the sin before God and man and complicates matters.

When repenting of a sin of the heart (for example, revengeful thoughts) you must seek God's forgiveness. When you commit outward transgressions (actually do something revengeful toward another), you must seek the forgiveness both from God and from the one against whom you transgressed.

True repentance for sin of the heart will forestall outward acts of sin. True repentance involves taking action to block further sin by radical amputation of all aids to sin and effort to plan ahead to do what is fine in the eyes of everyone (Rom. 12:17). At the time of repentance, action should also be taken to learn to say or do whatever it is that God requires in that situation rather than the sinful word or deed.

St. Augustine, in his discourse on the Lord's Prayer, said:

Or should the tempter set before you some woman of surpassing beauty; if chastity be within, iniquity without is overcome. Therefore, that he may not take you with the bait of a strange woman's beauty, fight with your own desire within; you have no physical perception of your enemy, but of your own concupiscence you do. You do not see the devil, but the object that engages you see. Get the mastery, then, over that which you are aware of within. Fight valiantly, for he who has regenerated you is your judge; he has arranged the lists, he is making ready the crown. But because you will without doubt be conquered if you have not him to aid you, if he abandon you: therefore say in prayer, "Lead us not into temptation."[4]

Augustine has put it well. In the same discourse, he continued:

I know that you have not yet understood me. Give me your attention, that you may understand. Suppose avarice tempts a man, and he is conquered in any single temptation (for sometimes even a good wrestler and fighter may get roughly handled): avarice, then, has got the better of a man, good wrestler though he be, and he has done some avaricious act. Or, there has been a passing desire; it has not brought the man to fornication, nor reached to adultery—for when this does take place, the man must at all events be kept back from the criminal act. But

[4]Augustine, "Discourse on the Lord's Prayer," Chauncey M. Depew, ed., *The Library of Oratory*, E.R. Du Mont Pub. Co., New York: 1902, p. 376. I have lightly modernized the quotation.

he "has seen a woman to lust after her": he has let his thoughts dwell on her with more pleasure than was right; he has allowed the attack, excellent combatant though he be, he has been wounded, but he has not consented to it [i.e., to the outward deed]; he has beaten back his emotional desire, has chastised it with the bitterness of grief; he has beaten it back and has prevailed. Still, in the very fact that he had slipped, has he ground for saying "Forgive us our debts."[5]

In these quotations, Augustine graphically depicts the inner/outer aspects of sin. He forcefully represents the struggle for mastery over one's desires that must be achieved. He is careful to point out that you cannot win this battle alone; you must seek the Spirit's strength to win over temptation. The words "fight with your own desire" are important. There is a struggle within that requires "valiant" fighting, as he puts it. Too often Christians think that merely passive faith or recognition of the victory of Christ by which we too are counted victorious in Him is sufficient. This sort of quietism has led many believers into despair. We are commanded to act, but not in our own strength. We are to obey all the Lord's commands, in the wisdom and power of the indwelling Spirit, who strengthens us to overcome sin by means of the Scriptures to which He enlightens us.

## Conclusion
In general, it is helpful to see sin spelled out as a process involving several stages, since at the inception of each, it becomes possible to cut short the process. For the believer, God

[5]*Ibid,* p. 377.

has already eliminated eternal death, the ultimate fruit of sin, so that our concern has focused on stages one, two, and three. You can guard against conceiving sin by using the Bible, just as Jesus did. And outer acts of sin can be aborted, even when you have sinned inwardly and conceived sin in your heart, by repentance and radical amputation. (This is the one abortion that must be urged upon every child of God.) From all of this we learn that God holds each one personally responsible for his thoughts, imagination, acts, and words, and will allow no blameshifting.

Have you been indulging in inner heart sin? Do you realize that unchecked and unrepented inner assent will, in time, give birth to outer transgression? Don't you recognize that even the inner assent is odious to God? No one else may know what goes on in your mind (Ps. 44:21), but God does. He is distinctly called the "Heart-Knower" (Acts 1:24). And He is concerned.

Christian, resist sin at the start, as Jesus did. Abort inner sin before it is born. Augustine encourages us with these words:

> Pray that God may make you conqueror of yourself . . . not of your enemy without, but of your own soul within. . . . Let no enemy from without be feared: conquer yourself, and the whole world is conquered.[6]

[6]*Ibid.*, pp. 379, 375.

# YOU CAN CONQUER DOUBT

Now James raises a complicating problem. In one sense, all of our difficulties with spiritual growth can be divided into two sorts: principal problems and complicating problems. A principal problem is one on which one's prime difficulty turns. A complicating problem, because of its association with the principal problem, makes it more difficult to solve. It thus so "complicates" the situation that often it is impossible to solve the principal problem without first solving the complicating problem (or, at least, working on the solution to both at once). And, interestingly, what may be a complicating problem for one person may be a principal problem for another.

Lack of self-discipline, for instance, is a typical complicating problem that may keep you from developing almost any pattern of life that God's Word requires. That is because regularity and consistency (the two basic characteristics of discipline) are essential for replacing sinful habits with their biblical alternatives. Thus, lack of self-discipline can defeat your attempt to control your mind—a crucial factor in dealing with desire as you have seen. Doubt, the subject of this chapter, also may become a complicating problem. The reason I make a point about complicating problems is because James presents doubts as such. When he says that if you lack wisdom (the principal problem), pray; but if you pray in a double-minded manner, don't expect God to give you wisdom. Attaining wisdom depends on removing doubt from prayer. Double-mindedness must be dealt with before you seek anything from God.

Now, of course, a complicating problem can become a principal problem; at times there may be no other problem in view. But, that happens only at its inception. It is of the nature of a complicating problem to eventually lead to other problems. In fact, it can become so all-pervasive that it can virtually tie up all progress in your spiritual life until, like a stalled vehicle on the highway clogging traffic, it is cleared away.

Generalizing from the way doubt blocks all access to wisdom, James says, "If you are double-minded, don't expect anything from God." Doubt ruins everything because it ruptures the relationship between you and your Lord. Moreover, by its pervasiveness, doubt adversely affects your whole life: you will become unstable in all your ways. So, far from treating a complicating problem casually, because it is "only a secondary problem," you must deal with the complicating problem immediately, urgently, because it stands in the way of all progress and causes immense harm. James writes:

> So, if any of you lacks wisdom, let him ask God for it, since He gives to everyone unreservedly and without reproaching, and it will be given to him. But let him ask in faith, without doubting, because a person who doubts is like a wave of the sea that is driven and tossed by the wind. That person shouldn't suppose that he will receive anything from the Lord, because a double-minded man is unstable in all of his ways (James 1:5-8).

## Doubt and Double-mindedness

I don't know how much difficulty you have with doubt, but James considers it prevalent enough to mention in two places in his book. Such a doubter (v. 6) is called "double-minded" (v. 8; literally, "double-souled"). Double-mindedness is the opposite of the *teleios* condition that James wants for you. He sees doubt as dividedness down deep within the soul. The *teleios* person is whole, integrated, complete, self-consistent. The double-minded individual cannot agree with himself. Today he is of one mind, tomorrow of another. Internally, he debates issues incessantly, never coming to firm decisions. He vascillates; he is "limping [between] two different opinions" leaning first one way then the other (1 Kings 18:21, RSV). He will not take a firm stand, declare his allegiance and stick to it.

At a baseball game, every time one team got a hit, scored a run, or made an outstanding play, a man in the back row cheered loudly. But every time the other team was successful, he cheered with equal vigor. During the seventh inning stretch, a woman standing in front of him turned around and said, "Sir, I don't mean to be nosey, but I can't help noticing that you root just as strongly for one team as you do for the other. I'm curious. How is that?"

"Well, I'll tell you," he replied, "I'm a farmer, I live way out in the boonies and I get to watch a game only once a year. At that one game, I'm gonna' be on the winning side!"

There are many people like that who hedge their bets. They are persons without loyalties, who blow here and there with the wind. These persons are divided between obedient action and acts of continued sin. They do an inordinate amount of talking to themselves. If you could listen to what they are saying, as God can, you would hear them telling themselves: *Should I divorce Wilbur on unbiblical grounds or not? Will God really do anything about it if I do? . . . Is God serious about church discipline? Do I have to go through that messy*

*process with Mary or would it be easier simply to leave the
church and find another? . . . Maybe homosexuality really isn't
a sin—even though the Bible treats it as such. . . . Does the
Bible have the answers to my relational problems as Paul
seems to say in 2 Timothy 3:15-17, or should I get the advice
of a psychotherapist as well?*

James depicts the double-minded as persons tossed with
inner turmoil and instability, an instability that, at length,
reaches its destructive hand into every area of life. But before
considering the effects of instability, let's take a closer look at
the turmoil itself. Surely, from what James has to say, one can
only conclude that this unsettled state is an agonizing, frustrat-
ing condition. Here is how James describes the inner turmoil
of the doubter:

> A person who doubts is like a wave of the sea that is
> driven and tossed by the wind (James 1:6).

We too use the expression "He wavers," when speaking of
one who takes an erratic, ever-changing course. The wave is an
appropriate analogy. What could be more unstable than a
wave? A wave is forever changing its size and shape. You can't
pin it down to any one configuration.

Moreover, the wave is at the mercy of outside influences, as
James notes: it is "driven," it is "tossed." It has no inner power
of direction. It does not propel itself. Today, the winds blow
this way or that and the wave moves under their influence.
Tomorrow it will all be different.

A double-minded person tends to be like the last person he
talked to. You never know what to expect of him. He is unpredictable. You never know what he will be like the next time
you meet him. And, sad to say, neither does *he* know what he
will be like or where he will be headed a month or, perhaps,
even a week from now. That is a frightful way to live: no

certainty, no loyalty, no direction, no stability. All is in flux; he lives a life of continuous confusion and disruption. Nothing is ever tacked down tightly.

I know a preacher who has adopted every fad he has been exposed to. At one time he became enamored with the puritan literature that began to be republished a few years back. He became a neo-puritan, adopting not only puritan concepts (some of which are excellent and some of which are dubious), but even speaking puritan language—for a while. Then, he discovered Robert Schuller. So, everything was changed: preaching, language, concepts—all went through a metamorphosis. Then, he changed again, and again, and again. Lately, he has taken up the practices of the church growth movement and has adopted some of the teachings of theonomy (a teaching which applies Old Testament Law to the U.S. government). This turmoil and change has adversely affected his ability to lead a flock. Indeed, dragging a congregation through his sudden shifts of thought and practice has proven too much for them. Not only has he lost members with each new allegiance, but he has been forced to change churches and denominations at various intervals. Despite his basically good gifts, excellent training, and solid opportunities, his ministry counts for little because of his double-mindedness. He lacks true leadership ability because, like a wave, he has no inner stability, direction, and power. He lacks the commitment to the Word necessary to stabilize his thinking and actions. He is at the mercy of the latest theological opinion.

## Faith

The inner dynamic, a mind James pictured tossed and driven, a soul unstable as a wave, leads to the tragic disruption of all of life. The doubter is afraid; he is unwilling to believe, to trust, to depend wholly on God and His Word; as James says, he lacks faith. That is why he is always looking for certainty but never finds it. Certainty never comes to those who lack faith. Certainty is not the ground, but the fruit of faith. Here is James' great insight: If you see someone who is unstable *generally* ("in all his ways"), you can look for double-mindedness behind his way of life.

Faith is absolutely essential to the complete life, the life that pleases God. The dire consequence of the life of doubt is spelled out: "That person shouldn't suppose that he will receive anything from the Lord" (James 1:7). This is true of salvation, and it is equally true of the Christian's life. Salvation is by grace, through *faith.* Later on in his letter James makes it clear that faith without works is dead (that isn't the kind of "faith" he is talking about here), but in this place, James just as plainly claims that works (of prayer, etc.) without faith are dead.

Faith pertains not only to salvation, but to everything in the Christian's life. Jesus says, "Believe . . . and you shall have" (Mark 11:24); here James says, "Doubt, and you won't." That is the flip side to keep in mind.

If your life is in turmoil, it may be the result of doubt. Ask yourself, *Do I really believe the Gospel? Am I sure I am saved?* If you are not sure of your salvation, then settle the matter before reading further. Recognize your sin and the judgment of God. Trust Christ as your Saviour. Believe that when He died on the cross He was taking the punishment for guilty sinners like you, and say to Him, "Lord, I believe You died for me." Rest your entire future welfare on Him. Depend on what He has done to deal with your sin and you will be saved.

If you are already a Christian, ask, "How dependable am I? Do I really believe God's promises enough to rely on them, whatever the outcome? Is my faith firm enough to know right from wrong and to enable me to disagree with others when necessary rather than be influenced by whatever I hear next? Or do I give equal time to what God says and to what the world teaches? Am I hedging my bets? Do I root for both teams? Am I one who lacks so much because I have no reason to "suppose that I should receive anything from the Lord"?

If you lack faith, then it is likely that you have not been reading the Scriptures enough or rightly.[1] You may not have been attending a Bible-teaching church regularly where you can learn God's will and the certainty of His promises. The reason I suggest these two possible reasons for your lack of faith is because God works faith in the heart through His Word: "Faith comes by hearing and hearing through the Word of Christ" (Rom. 1:17). Faith is being sure of God; but you cannot be sure of Him if you don't know what He says. If you lack faith, examine your priorities and find time for regular, in-depth study of the Scriptures and for hearing the regular, faithful preaching of God's Word. After all, faith is so essential that it is impossible to please God without it (Heb. 11:6).

## Instability

All of your life will be affected if you are a double-minded doubter. But what is this instability of which James writes? The word *unstable*, in the original, refers to "disruption, disorder, turmoil and confusion." Hence, the image of the tossed and driven wave so aptly fits. Agitated, aimless, purposeless living is what James is talking about.

Such agitated living also keeps everyone around you in a stir. Your family can't depend on you; you will let the church

[1]For a system of practical (rather than abstract) Bible study, see my book *What to do on Thursday*. Presbyterian and Reformed Pub. Co., Phillipsburg, NJ: 1982. The idea in the title is that to study the Bible properly, you must learn how to use what you learn not only on Sunday, to pass the next Bible quiz, but on Thursday (and every other day in the week).

down; you are likely to lose jobs because of your fickleness and indecision; etc. Because of instability, you become a liability to everyone, including yourself.

If you are uncertain about God's promises, then you will be disobedient to His commands. What God commands is not always easy; the repercussions of obedience in a world opposed to God are not always pleasant. Obviously, then, faithfulness depends on the certainty of your commitment to God and to the Scriptures. Doubters do not have what it takes to obey; they continually fudge. Many of them are under the misapprehension that the old axiom, "Half a loaf is better than none," pertains as well to matters of faith as to anything else. But that isn't so. God will not share His glory with another. Elijah said, "If the Lord is God, follow Him; but if it is Baal, follow him" (1 Kings 18:21, MLB). Don't try to root for both sides.

If God says that you may not get a divorce on grounds other than He allows, then that is final. Stop playing around with the possibility. It is out of the question. Get rid of the "ifs and buts and maybes." Instead, get to work doing whatever is necessary to make your marriage succeed. If the Scriptures teach that it is time to institute church discipline, then so be it. Forget the messy times that may lie ahead. Stop thinking that if you do nothing, the problem may vanish; it won't. Instead, study carefully Christ's directions in Matthew 18:15ff (and elsewhere) and do what is necessary. Dismiss the temptation to run away from your problem by moving to another church. God has spoken. Who are you to doubt the wisdom of His Word?

But, you see, the double-minded doubter will not have it that way. And, he is aided and abetted by those who declare the clear directions of Scripture "too simplistic" to follow merely as they are set forth. They must have things more complex. Much so-called scholarship, and a good bit of the leadership in the church today, appears to be the fruit of double-mindedness. Certainly there are difficulties, but God's Word is clear enough for the simple, sincere student to discover His will and, in faith, live by it. God does not want believers tripping over their own feet, contradicting themselves at every turn, and living inconsistent, zigzag lives.

Double-mindedness is the source of much of the weakness and confusion in the church today, probably a great deal more than we realize. If James' words about instability depict your life, then your problem is probably doubt. If it is, you'd better do something about it—quickly!

### How to Solve the Problem

"I think James is talking about me," you say. "Down inside I find doubts and fears and my life certainly isn't stable. But what can I do about my double-minded lack of faith?" I have already mentioned the importance of faithful, practical Bible study of the proper sort, and the regular attendance upon the preaching of the Scriptures. But there are other factors involved. James takes up the problem of doubt once more. This time, he addresses the doubter directly:

> Draw near to God and He will draw near to you. Wash your hands, you sinners, and purify your hearts, you double-minded persons. Be distressed, and sorrow and cry; let your laughter be turned to sorrow and your gladness to dejection. Be humbled before the Lord and He will exalt you (James 4:8-10).

When you read the Bible, including these verses, you will discover God's solution to the problem. And you will find that the Bible also helps you to follow whatever requirements God proposes as the means to the solution.

To find relief from doubt and the turmoil it generates, you must recognize that such double-minded doubt is not merely an intellectual issue; it is a moral problem.[2] It is always a moral issue to doubt God—either His wisdom or truth. It is a moral problem when you claim to believe in Him, then hedge your bets by sidling up in a cozy manner to someone else.

Moreover, faith, and faithful prayer, evaporate when there is unconfessed sin in your life, when you toy with sin (or the possibility of sinning), when you muddle God's commands with all sorts of unbiblical qualifications and when you rationalize disobedience. These are the things that the double-minded doubter does.

Since double-mindedness is sin, the solution lies in repentance. That is what James teaches (4:8-10). He issues an urgent command to repent. If you are a doubter of the sort he describes, then his directions pertain to you. There are three things that you must do.

1. You must recognize that you have been straying from God. The farther one roams from Him the more confused he becomes. So, "draw near" to God in prayer. Reestablish friendship with God: "Friendship with the world is enmity with God" (4:4). You have allowed worldly thoughts, values, and practices to guide you. More and more you have found yourself confused over the antithesis between God's ways and the world's (see Isa. 55:8-9). You have learned to like what the world promotes, much of which you are pretty sure God doesn't approve. So, you've tried to "integrate" the two, but you found they didn't fit and the world's ways more often than

---

[2]There is, of course, a healthy sort of uncertainty that one maintains as he searches the Scriptures for God's truth. This benign skepticism in Berean-like persons is commended by Luke as "noble" (Acts 17:11). But note the difference. On the one hand, uncertainty remains only until God's will is ascertained. On the other, it is this very will, once discerned, that is questioned and doubted!

not win out. You read your Bible less and less because it reminds you of your sin. You come near to God less frequently because you are guilty of adultery with the world (James 4:4). No wonder you are confused, in turmoil, double-minded! James says, "All this must cease!" That is the first thing you must do: recognize how far you have strayed from your Heavenly Father.

2. When you draw near to God, confess your sin humbly before Him and ask Him to forgive you. Some say that once you have been forgiven you never again need to ask God's forgiveness for sin. When you sin you say, "Thank You, Lord, that it's all under the blood" and walk happily on your way. Is that what James is saying? Of course not!

It is true that Christ's work on the cross leads to a once-for-all *judicial* forgiveness. God doesn't haul you into court again every time you sin. You don't get saved all over again. But, that is judicial forgiveness—forgiveness before God *as Judge*. There is another forgiveness of which Jesus spoke: *Fatherly* forgiveness. This second form of forgiveness, to which James also alludes, is fully described in the Lord's Prayer where Jesus taught us to pray to the Father, "Forgive us our trespasses" (Matt. 6:12). This, He says, in response to the disciples' request for a model of regular prayer, should always characterize prayer: "When you pray, say. . . ." Moreover, this is the only one of the several petitions in the Lord's Prayer that Jesus develops. In doing so, He says:

> Now if you forgive people their trespasses against you, so too your heavenly Father will forgive you; but if you won't forgive people, neither will your Father forgive you your trespasses (Matt. 6:14-15).

Notice how the Lord's Prayer is addressed to the Father, and that in speaking of God's forgiveness of His children's sins, Jesus mentions the Father twice as Forgiver (vv. 14-15). Surely, then, while judicial forgiveness, determining your eternal destiny, is a once-for-all matter, fatherly forgiveness, determining your closeness to and fellowship with the Father, is not. Instead, it is a regular, ongoing matter.

3. You must take this matter of repentance seriously and with all urgency respond to James' command. Those words in James 4:9 are not calling for an emotional eruption on your part (though that might well occur spontaneously at times). What James is describing is genuine repentance and concern. The kind that shakes a person out of his lethargy, that makes him sorry for what he has done. Mainly, he stresses serious concern and urgency.

James says, Once you recognize the problem, don't let any grass grow under your feet; solve it—now! Don't let any distraction turn you from your resolve to draw near to God. Forget TV, cancel your dinner engagement, if necessary. Let your distress over your offense against God turn you from any and all pleasures that might cover up the gravity of the situation until you have settled the matter and stand in the proper relationship to God once more. Seek God's forgiveness ("purify your hearts"), seek the forgiveness of any others you may have wronged, and right all wrongs ("wash your hands"). Acknowledge that you have sinned. And, once again, God will draw near to you in paternal fellowship. Repent of your fickleness toward God, of your doubts about His wisdom, of your unwillingness to follow Christ wholeheartedly, and in full faith commit all your ways to Him.

# F I V E

# YOU CAN PRAY
# EFFECTIVELY

Frequently, Christian counselors hear the protest, "I've prayed about it and nothing happened." I've learned to look the protester straight in the eye and reply, "Well, what's so unusual about that?" Then there follows a discussion of the fact that much (perhaps most) prayer is wasted, ineffectual, or answered negatively. When people hear this, they are usually amazed to learn that what they thought was virtually an automatic process is, in fact, anything but.

Perhaps you too need instruction about prayer. Possibly you are startled to hear that prayer can be wasted. While he didn't say everything that could be said, James is surely the one to teach you about it. In his many comments on prayer, James focuses on the inner aspects of prayer: the attitudes and spiritual condition of the one who prays. Perhaps more than any other writer of Scripture, James reveals the unsettling facts about wasted prayer.

It is amazing to discover how many people think that God is obligated to answer their prayers, how many of those think He is obligated to answer positively, and, of those, how many think He is obligated to answer *their way,* on *their terms,* according to *their schedules.* Such thinking, James makes clear, is all wrong. One major task that James undertakes is to straighten out fuzzy thinking about prayer. He wants to do this, because the magical views that many Christians entertain about prayer keep them from becoming complete persons. And some, discouraged by not receiving answers to prayer, when they were led to believe that they should, have all but given up on prayer, if not on their faith.

## Wasted Prayer

If all the prayers offered by millions of Christians around the world on any given day were effective, there would be a vast transformation on earth in no time. How can you believe that most prayer is effective when no such thing happens? The fact of the matter is that either there is much ineffective, wasted prayer or the promises of God concerning prayer are false. Since Christians don't allow the latter conclusion, it seems that there is only one conclusion—a lot of prayer is wasted.

The Bible frequently speaks of wasted prayer. Far from being a shock, the fact ought to be a well-known truism among believers. Look for a moment at a few examples.

In Proverbs 15:29, we read, "The Lord is far from the wicked but He hears the prayer of the righteous" (MLB). Here, in unmistakable terms, God says that prayers of the unsaved will not be answered. Jews in Christ's time understood this (John 9:31). Unbelievers have no rights at the throne of grace. Access to God was opened by Jesus, but only for those who believe (see also Prov. 1:28; 15:8; 21:27).

Luke records Jesus' parable of the Pharisee and the tax collector. There our Lord makes the point that the self-righteous Pharisee "prayed to himself" (Luke 18:11). His prayer never reached God. It was like a balloon that ascended to the ceiling of the temple and stuck there. His prayer failed because it was not really a prayer at all; it was a self-righteous recital of his own good works.

In 1 Peter 3:7 God makes it clear that He doesn't listen to the prayers of Christian husbands who treat their wives poorly. A good relationship with God is dependent on a good relationship with one's wife. Communication with God depends on good family communication. The husband must see that he is reconciled to his wife and maintains a good relationship with her. Otherwise, Peter writes, "Your prayers will be interrupted," presumably until such a time as the husband/wife relationship is repaired (cf. Mal. 2:13-14 for an instance of this very thing in Israel). Just think about the many Christian husbands or wives who have refused to resolve their problems and still expect answers to their prayers. Incidentally, it will do counselors no good to advise those having marriage difficulties to "pray about your problem." That's just it—they are in no condition to pray effectively. Unless their prayers are prayers of confession and repentance, followed by willingness to make changes for the future, those prayers are wasted.

In the Bible any number of conditions for successful praying are set forth. For instance, God says that whoever refuses to heed the cry of the poor will not be heard when he cries out to God (Prov. 21:13). God considers the prayer of those who turn away from hearing His law "an abomination" (Prov. 28:9). The psalmist declares, "If I regard iniquity in my heart, the Lord will not hear" (Ps. 66:18, MLB). After looking at James' comments on temptation and sinning in the heart, think how many prayers are wasted because of the sinful inner condition of those who pray! Along the same lines, consider these words of God to sinning Israel: "When you make many prayers I will not hear" (Isa. 1:15, KJV). "Your iniquities have separated between you and your God . . . [so] that He will not hear you" (Isa. 59:2, KJV). Take special note of the fact that *many* of their prayers were wasted—because of unrepentant sin. Couldn't the same thing be true today?

James also has something to say about wasted prayer. We've already learned that the double-minded doubter can expect nothing from God when he prays: "That person shouldn't suppose that he will receive anything from the Lord" (1:7). Those who lack faith waste prayer (v. 6). Later on, James writes: "You don't have because you don't ask! You don't receive when you do ask, since you ask wrongly—to waste it on your pleasures" (4:2-3). Plainly, James did not expect all prayers to be answered; there is strong evidence to the contrary.

### Encouragement to Pray

I have alluded to only *some* of the pitfalls in prayer; but even those are formidable! Others will become apparent when we study the qualifications and requirements for effective prayer that James sets forth.

"Well," you say, "I'm discouraged! If much, perhaps most, prayer is unheard,[1] then what's the use of praying; mine probably won't be heard either. The averages are against it." Wrong! Through James God *encourages* you to pray.

Good college football teams usually come from big universities. But good basketball teams often come from the smaller colleges. Prayer is like basketball. You don't have to be an Elijah or an Apostle Paul to pray effectively. Indeed, when James holds up the prayer of Elijah as an example (James 5:17-18), he points out that Elijah was a human being just like you, with the same emotional makeup and the same difficulties you have. In spite of much failure, you are in the running;

[1] That is, unheeded. Of course, God is aware of every prayer that is prayed; in that sense He "hears" them all (otherwise the prayer of the wicked would not be an "abomination" to Him). And He hears even before they are uttered (Isa. 65:24).

effective prayer *is* possible. It is not beyond you at all.

In his discussion of wisdom, James tells those who lack wisdom to "ask God for it, since He gives to everyone unreservedly and without reproaching, and it will be given" (James 1:5). Those words are intended to encourage you to pray.

James encourages prayer *by urging you to pray for what you lack:* "If any of you lack wisdom, *let him ask.*" Solomon asked for wisdom and discernment, and got it (1 Kings 3:9). And because he asked rightly—not to waste it on himself, but in order to honor God and govern His people well—God gave him "exceedingly, abundantly above all he could ask or think" (see 1 Kings 3:12-14).

James encourages prayer *by promising that God will give you what you lack:* "It will be given to him" (1:5). It is not that God doesn't want you to have things, or that He is stingy; that isn't why so much prayer fails. The problem is that He wants to give more than you want to receive. This promise, "it will be given to him," like those in John 14:13-14, etc., however, must not be taken by itself, unqualified. God *will* answer, He *will* give—if and when you comply with His conditions. He is the One who sets the terms, not you or I.

One of the conditions is found in James 1:6: "But let him ask in faith, without doubting." God *promises* to give you all you need to become a *teleios* person. He promises to give nothing else. If you don't become complete, it is your fault. Either you haven't asked for what you need, or you haven't asked rightly.

James also encourages prayer *by making it clear how God gives:* "unreservedly and without reproaching" (v. 5). He gives graciously. The first of these two words means "simply, without reserve, with no strings attached." There are no conditions attached to God's gifts. He gives simply; that is, He simply gives—without further ado. The second encouraging description of God's giving is that He gives "without reproaching."

How often have you received something you would almost rather not have received because of the way in which it was given? The giver surprised you with some stinging remark or reminded you of what happened the last time he gave you something. No, there is none of that when God gives.

There is no reason for hesitating, no reason to fear asking. James' words are a great comfort to reluctant or guilty children who are not sure of their ground with the Father. The ground for approaching God boldly, without fear, is the finished, complete work of Jesus Christ. That's why you pray in Jesus' name. James' words should encourage you to pray. God promises to answer and assures you He will not give reproachingly or with strings attached. What more could you want? Why then are you hesitant to pray? What keeps your prayers from being answered? How does what you pray hamper the effectiveness of your prayers? We must answer those questions to the extent that James does.

## How to Pray

Prayer for wisdom (or anything else) is essential, but certain conditions are attached to prayer. When you fail to meet these conditions, don't expect God to give you what you request (James 1:7). Remember, *man*—not God— is always the problem when prayer is wasted.

James' list of conditions is not exhaustive, but the important thing to see is that James focuses on those that pertain to the heart. The sum of what he shows you is that God is concerned about your attitudes, your spiritual condition, and your relationship to Himself. Thus, again, James looks within and asks pertinent questions about the inner dynamics of effective prayer.

Prayer is not a bag of techniques, not learning the right formula, possessing some magic charm, or tacking on an opensesame type password like "in Jesus' name." It is not a matter of going through the proper rituals, nor agonizing before God for long periods of time or anything of the sort. No, the essential conditions to fulfill have to do with your heart.

James alludes to four essential conditions that must be met when praying. They are:
- Asking in faith (1:5-7);
- Asking for the right reason (4:2-3);
- Asking earnestly and specifically (5:16-17);
- Asking when in the proper relationship to God (5:16).

### Asking in Faith

There is no need to develop this matter fully since in the discussion of the double-minded doubter, whose attitude is just the opposite of an attitude of faith, we talked about faith. Perhaps, however, one or two additional remarks will help.

Faith is not mere assent. It certainly involves knowledge of what God promises and a belief that these promises are true. In these respects, the double-minded doubter already falls short, because he is not sure. That's why he hedges his bets, roots for both teams, and straddles the fence. But all of this comes out most clearly when we mention the third element of faith. In addition to knowledge and assent, there must be *trust*.

It was not enough for Elijah to proclaim "Jehovah, not Baal, is God!" The people had to follow up that affirmation by relinquishing *all* dependence upon Baal (prayers, customs, altars, groves, paraphernalia connected with Baal worship: all must go). And they needed to trust (rely, depend) *solely* on Jehovah and wholeheartedly worship Him.

To believe, in the biblical sense, is to turn from idols to serve the living and true God (1 Thes. 1:9). Idols, in our culture today, largely consist of viewpoints, ideologies, practices, movements, or persons that we depend on when we ought to depend on God. If, for example, God's Word tells you not to sue another believer, but instead work through church discipline to adjudicate matters (1 Cor. 6), it is less than dependence on God to retain a lawyer as a "backup" while pursuing church discipline. Action like that reveals an inner attitude of doubt and distrust in God.

Faith, then, is trust, dependence, and reliance on God and His Word. It is manifested in prayer when you really *depend* on God to answer. Dependence means that should God fail, you would fail with Him. You rely so completely on God that you close all other doors, burn all other bridges.

That kind of faith is an essential condition of prayer. The double-minded doubter wonders whether prayer will work. "So, just in case it doesn't . . . ," he says, "I'll . . . " and then he names some current rabbit's foot in which he will place his trust along with God. But that something else is an *idol*. It is put on an equal level with God—he trusts in both. In the end, the rabbit's foot takes God's place because He will not share His glory with another (Isa. 42:8; 48:11). God departs, and, at length, the rabbit's foot proves ineffectual.

So, then, faith means depending solely on God and His Word.

"But, if I pray for the healing of my daughter, shouldn't I also call the doctor? What do you mean by 'solely' depending on God and His Word?"

Yes, you should call the doctor if she is seriously ill—*because* you depend on God, not in spite of that fact. You depend on God by praying and by using medical means *because* in His Word God tells you to do both (James 5:14).[2] Let's put

---

[2]The word translated *anoint* in v. 14 should be "rub or smear." In chapter 14 I shall explain why.

it this way: Christ told us to pray, "Give us this day our daily bread." You do so. Does that mean that you may now sit under a palm tree and wait for a loaf to float out of the sky on a parachute? Certainly not. Prayer in faith doesn't mean inaction.

To depend on God's Word, means to depend on *all* He teaches and commands. To depend on God in prayer means to pray for your bread, *and*, as He requires, work for it as well (2 Thes. 3:10). You are trusting God to answer your prayer in the manner He has specified. If God says, "Pray and use medicine," then you must trust Him enough to do both. To only pray for bread or healing at first seems to involve greater faith. But it doesn't. It becomes a kind of double-mindedness in which you rely on a prayer-alone rabbit's foot of your own devising while claiming (wrongly) to depend on the God who expressly declares that He gives bread (healing or whatever) by the means commanded in His Word.

When you pray for daily bread, in effect, you are asking God for the opportunity, wisdom, strength, health, and whatever else is necessary to earn your bread *in accordance with His Word.* That, not some seemingly more pious way, is God's way; it is the way of faith.

### Asking for the Right Reason

> You desire something and don't have it. . . . You don't have because you don't ask! You don't receive when you do ask, since you ask wrongly—to waste it on your pleasures (James 4:2-3).

Notice that James is discussing *desire* here, not need. I have already distinguished these words and the concepts they represent, so I shall say nothing more about that. But, perhaps it is important to observe that for James, the issue is precisely *not* a matter of need.

James says one problem is failure to ask: "You don't have because you don't ask" (4:2). Certainly asking is the fundamental condition of effective prayer: one can't expect anything he doesn't ask for. That is not to say that God is not better to His children than they are to themselves and that He doesn't give them good things even when they don't ask. But it is true that you don't have because you fail to pray and that you have no right to *expect* something for which you fail to ask. God doesn't want you to take Him for granted.

There are those who question the need to ask. "Why should I? God already knows my needs and desires." Yes, of course He does, but, nevertheless, *He* has told you to ask and has made the reception of what you need and want largely dependent on asking.

Why? Perhaps, in part, He requires prayer so you will not take Him for granted. Perhaps for your own benefit. It is one way of reminding you of your utter dependence on Him. If all were provided automatically, as a sinner, taking God's provisions for granted, you'd soon forget the Source of your blessings.

Certainly, if asking is the condition for receiving, and, in turn, if the conditions for receiving resolve themselves into righteous inner spiritual attitudes and motives and a proper relationship to God, prayer is a strong incentive to live righteously. Indeed, many things seem to be tied into prayer this way, even the welfare of marriage (1 Peter 3:7).

Perhaps God requires prayer because He delights in your asking. I can know God's reasons for anything only insofar as He reveals them and, to my knowledge, a full rationale for prayer is not found in the Bible. The conjectures that I have been making are based solely upon biblical hints, nothing more. But, the command to pray and conditions for effective prayer are clearly set forth in Scripture.

The second reason for ineffective prayer that James mentions in this passage is failure to pray for the right reason (4:3). God doesn't answer selfish, hedonistic prayer (*pleasures* in verse 3 is the word from which our term "hedonism" comes). When you pray merely, or even first, for your wants, for *your own pleasure*, God will not answer your prayer.

Does that mean you should never ask for what you want? No, it doesn't mean that. But it does mean (1) you must want the right things (whatever is biblically allowable) and (2) you must ask for the right reason (ultimately, that is, to please God). What is wrong, foolish, or impossible is not a fit subject for prayer. You may pray for what is good and what is right *only* when you put pleasing God, thereby, before pleasing self. That is what is involved in Christ's own prayer, "Yet, don't do what I want but what You want" (Matt. 26:39). The desired boon, if granted, ought to be sincerely desired to please and honor God, *before* all else. If it is a blessing to others and also pleasing to you, fine. If God answers your prayer with a "no" (and that *is* an answer, don't forget) then, if you have put pleasing God first you should not be greatly disappointed. Moreover, the part of your prayer in which you asked, "Yet, do what You want," *will* have been answered affirmatively.

James talks about this from another angle when discussing the merchant planning his itinerary. He says that the merchant ought to say "If the Lord wills. . . ." We shall come to this passage in a later chapter, but, for now, note that James presupposes that the righteous merchant will prayerfully plan, asking, nevertheless, that God's will be done.

God abhors self-centered prayer. The Lord's Prayer begins with God, not with man and sets the tone for all that follows. Were God to grant many of your requests (asked from selfish motives) you would waste what He gives. Because you wanted it for yourself, that's how you would use it. But, you see, God wants you to use all you are and all you have for Him. This condition vividly teaches that truth. If you pray rightly, there is a greater likelihood that you will use what you get as you should: out of love for God and your neighbor rather than for yourself.

In this self-centered age and country, in which self-interest is justified by all sorts of specious arguments—even in the church—the requirement to consider our motives for praying is most helpful. Otherwise, there would be little to keep you from wasting what you receive. As it is, the condition makes you stop and think before praying. Indeed, it provides a restraint on self-interest and a check on avaricious attitudes. It is a very great blessing. It forces you to think and act as a Christian should.

### Ask Specifically and Earnestly

The petition of a righteous person has very powerful effects. Elijah was a man with the same sort of difficulties that we have, but he prayed earnestly that it might not rain, and for three years and six months it didn't rain on the earth. Then he prayed and the sky gave rain and the earth brought forth its fruit (James 5:16-18).

Again, in 5:15, James emphasizes the importance of believing prayer, and connects it with the healing of the sick. Then, as an encouragement to trust God and to show the greatness of the power that God releases in answer to believing prayer, James mentions Elijah's prayers. In doing so, he calls his prayer "petition" (v. 16) and says that Elijah "prayed earnestly." Here, James implies two conditions for effective prayer:

• prayer must be specific and concrete.
• prayer must be earnest or fervent.

Concrete, specific prayer (*deesis*) arises from a sense of lack.

Usually the *deesis* is uttered in the warmth of desire. It is the kind of specific and concrete prayer that a missionary prays when he asks specifically for the needed Landrover that will enable him to carry the Gospel out into the bush. It is occasional and therefore to be distinguished from formal routinized prayer.

Elijah's prayer was earnest (v. 17). In describing it, James uses one of the few full Hebraisms found in the New Testament. Literally, he says, "In (or with) prayer, he prayed," using an intensive form, that denoted earnestness. The Hebrew form, reproduced here in Greek, is most nearly expressed by our phrase "He *really* prayed." That is why the *King James Version* calls it *fervent* prayer.


## Ask in Proper Relationship to God

We come now to the heart of everything James says about the inner dynamics of prayer. "The petition of a righteous person has very powerful effects" (v. 16).

The righteous person is (1) one who is justified (declared righteous in God's sight) by faith in Christ and, here, (2) is living righteously (i.e., in accordance with God's Word).

God is not a cosmic dispensing machine. Prayer is not a matter of putting "prayer quarters" in, pushing the right button, and retrieving the gift that rolls into the opening slot. Too often prayer is viewed that way. No, prayer is one person asking another Person for something. God is a Person, not a machine, or an impersonal force.

You don't even ask your earthly father, who loves you, for something when your relationship with him is bad. First, the relationship must be right.

God is not obligated to answer your prayers *when* you want, the *way* you want, or according to *your* terms. He is a Person, and because of the kind of Person He is, He sets the terms and conditions for prayer. Indeed, if He had not invited us to pray and encouraged us to do so, in the name of His Son, we, sinful sons that we are, might not have dared to come into His Presence. But, He has urged us to come "boldly before the throne of grace" (Heb. 4:16). Yet, we must come as righteous persons (right, according to His requirements). Many of the unrighteous ways that hinder prayer have already been mentioned: unconfessed sin, double-mindedness, refusal to grant forgiveness to others, wrong relationships, self-centeredness (see Ps. 24:3-6). But, in general, what God requires is genuine petition, *from the heart*, that first asks, "Forgive me my trespasses." Requests should be made humbly, in repentance (when necessary), thanking God for the promise of forgiveness that He so graciously extends.

James shows us that prayer is accepted not because of pious positions of the body or hands, not because of proper ritualistic formulas, but because a righteous person prays God's way, out of godly motives, for those things that are biblically legitimate. In essence, effective prayer is a matter of the heart.

# YOU CAN HAVE
# GOOD MOTIVES

"He's been lying to me! He got a raise and didn't tell me about it. I'd have never known if I hadn't found that check. But what I'd like to know now is what he's been doing with that extra money these four months. The only thing I can think of is that there must be another woman. Oh! What am I going to do?"

"Well, how about it Sam? Is Brenda right? What about the raise?"

"Pastor, yes, she's right. I did get a raise, and I didn't tell her about it. But there's no other woman."

"OK, then, can you explain?"

"Do I have to?"

"It seems wise."

"Alright, if you think so. But I hate to do it. [Taking out his wallet] Look, I've got it all here. I've been saving up to take Brenda on a two-week vacation to Cancun. I've got it all arranged with the travel agent and all I need is one more month's pay to pull it off. Now the surprise is ruined."

That scenario might serve as an example of several things,

not the least of which is the problem of judging (usually misjudging) another's motives. James has some important words to speak on the subject.

In chapter 2, James deals with the sin of favoritism (vv. 1-13). His special concern is favoritism shown because of money. Basically, he teaches that from God's perspective poverty is no evil and riches are no advantage. Because money doesn't influence God, it should not influence us either. The poor Christian should boast about his riches in Christ as the child of the King. At the same time, James directs the rich Christian to recognize his utter poverty apart from Christ. He should focus on the true riches in Christ, humbling himself and recognizing that whatever present possessions he has are temporary. Both the rich and the poor stand equal before God and should be viewed the same by us. James is concerned to change wrong perspectives both of the rich and the poor in the church by helping them see themselves from God's perspective.

In the discussion of poverty and riches, when emphasizing the temptation to kowtow to a rich man, James sketches an all-too typical scene. He draws the verbal picture of a rich visitor in shining clothes entering the assembly of believers. This man is shown special attention because of his riches, while a poor visitor is neglected (2:1-10). Then, he puts it straight to the reader, telling him such discrimination comes from judging with "evil thoughts" (v. 4). Any judge who allows judgment to be perverted because of a person's wealth is counted an evil judge. So too when believers discriminate between those who are rich and poor, they do so from "evil thoughts" (or *motives*). The motive in the instance sketched is to obtain some advantage from the wealthy visitor and, perhaps, at the same time, to avoid any trouble he might cause. The motive would be avarice or fear or a combination of both.

This motive, on the part of those who show favoritism might not even be personal. They might genuinely have the welfare of the church in mind, hoping for no personal benefit. On the other hand, motives might be mixed. Either way, James condemns the practice of preferential treatment on the basis of one's financial status or position of authority. It is wrong, he contends, because such treatment stems from "evil" motives ("thoughts or reasonings").

Because motives involve an inner process of reasoning, James calls on the reader to think carefully about favoritism. He shows that it is both wrong and foolish:

1. Because it is totally out of sync with the expressed will of God (Lev. 19:15, 18).

2. Because it divides the body (James 2:4).

3. Because the one showing favoritism takes it on himself to determine who is most important.

4. Because it hurts the poor by dishonoring them, it hurts the rich by losing your good influence with them, and it hurts the work of Christ by misrepresenting God before men (v. 6).

5. Because it is foolish to despise those whom God loves (v. 5), to honor those who despise you (v. 6), and to honor those who despise God (v. 7).

These arguments should lead you to repent and to think more clearly about your motives if you have been guilty of showing favoritism. Obviously, James wants you to examine your motives if you have fallen into this sin.

But it is just because James is concerned about motives— the inner reasons for your outer actions—that he cannot stop with saying what he has said so far. James points out that motives may be *misread*. That is why he urges you to carefully examine your motives. This concern comes out especially in verse 8: "If you really fulfill the royal law, which according to the Scripture is, 'You must love your neighbor as yourself,' you do well." James points out that it is possible to show special concern for a rich person out of a good motive that corresponds to the law of love. You must be careful to examine your motives because, regardless of what others may say or think, it is all too easy for others, and even you, yourself, to misread your motives.

The tendency, of course, is to call your own sins something less than sin: a "need" (when it is really a desire), an "illness" (when it is a moral issue), etc. The problem must be dealt with continually. But it is just as common to call another's actions sinful when they are not (that's what Job's counselors did). Those who are concerned to be biblical may easily fall into this temptation. It is easy to do so, not only because of the sinful propensities that remain, but also because it is easy to identify as sin something that, on the surface looks like sin, but isn't. This great error comes from judging motives.

## Judging Motives

Lay it down as a rule never to be deviated from: It is not your province to judge another's motive. It is hard enough to accurately judge your own. God did not assign you the task of judging another's motives. It is not possible for you to do so. The Bible consistently teaches that judging motives—i.e., determining the reason for what one does—is an activity that belongs to God alone. He has reserved this task for Himself because no one else can read the mind and the heart of another.

"Man looks on the outward appearance, but the Lord looks on the heart" (1 Sam. 16:7, MLB). Here the two tasks and capabilities are clearly differentiated. God is called the "Heart-knower" (Acts 1:24). Referring to reading another's heart, in the utter frustration of a human being attempting the impossible, Jeremiah asks, "Who can know it?" God's answer is "I the Lord search the heart" (Jer. 17:9-10, KJV). Your task, then, is to treat a person according to his actions and his words; you must *never* try to determine his motives.

How frequently husbands and wives attempt the impossible. That is why Brenda, rather than giving Sam the benefit of the doubt, ruined a perfectly good surprise: she tried—and failed—to judge his motives. Husbands and wives will tell their pastor in counseling, "I know he/she won't do it; he/she doesn't mean what he/she says." Parents judge the thoughts of their children rather than asking them to explain their reasons for some action. Churches sometimes hesitate to receive repentant members back into full fellowship because, they say, "We are not sure he is repentant." To determine such things is God's business; it isn't yours, the church's, or anyone else's.


## What Looks Like Sin
There is a good reason why God has not assigned the task of judging the motives of another to sinful, fallible human beings. What looks like sin may not be. Despite the strong language James uses to condemn favoritism, and the amount of space he devotes to denouncing all such practices, he does pull aside from his thought for a moment to make an important parenthetical qualification (2:8). Here he says that it is possible to show concern for a rich person in a way that looks exactly like favoritism but is not. This seemingly suspicious concern may, in fact, be entirely proper and lawful.

Indeed, James implies that identical actions may be taken from very different (even opposite) motives. It is conceivably possible that in order to fulfill the royal law of love—because your motive is love—you might show special concern to a rich man, escorting him to a good seat, just as (at another time) you might do the same for a poor man. In other words, your obvious concern for him may not flow from motives of advantage at all, but, let us say, from a desire for him to hear the Gospel and be saved. If you knew the rich man was hard of hearing, this would be a thoughtful act on your part. But, to others, who did not know that fact, it might look like an act of favoritism. This would be a natural assumption because such things are usually done out of evil motives. But no one has the right to assume anything about another's motives. James' important point, then, is that all that glitters is not pyrite. There is some gold in the world after all!

Just as it is easy in a world of sin to read history with a jaundiced eye, debunking all patriotism and heroism as acts motivated by personal gain, so too is it easy for Christians to become overly skeptical about the kindly acts of fellow-believers. When you know the jumble of motives that you often find inside yourself, it is not hard to become cynical and attribute seemingly good actions to evil motives. Perhaps you have fallen into such thinking patterns. If so, you can see how great a temptation it is to attribute actions to bad motives when the Bible itself identifies the very action as one which frequently does stem from such motives. That is the case here, and that is why James is insistent on his qualification being heard.

It is important to learn to counter all cynical evaluations of others. This is done when one learns, in love, to "believe all things and hope all things" about another's actions. That important guideline found in 1 Corinthians 13:7 means that until the facts prove otherwise, you must *always* give your brothers and sisters the benefit of any doubt. You must attribute the highest motives to them. That is an important policy for you to follow because you really are incapable of judging the motives of another's heart.

But as important as that consideration might be, it is not really the major concern here. Rather, James focuses most of his attention on the one performing the act. He is interested in getting him to examine his own motives. Look once more at those words: "If you really fulfill the royal law . . . you do well."

In a sense the word *really* is the key. "In spite of all outward appearances," James says, "I realize your concern for the rich man may be genuine." Your actions toward him may well be an instance of fulfilling the royal (preeminent) law of love. If so, your outward actions toward the unbelieving rich man are good: "you do well."

Perhaps, as I suggested, the unbelieving rich man is hard of hearing, so out of purely evangelistic motives, you make it a point to find him a good seat where he can hear easily. That is "doing well," because what you do flows from loving rather than selfish motives. But others, not knowing his problem, may misinterpret your actions as favoritism. They are not to do so; nor are you to hesitate to do the good thing out of fear that they will.

## Being Misunderstood

It is not pleasant to be misunderstood or to be accused of something that you never intended at all. I remember once being accused of playing up to a seminary audience when I know that behind my words was no such motivation whatsoever. I was shocked at the accusation because, if anything, I am usually accused of the opposite. In fact, I was so startled that I was speechless. But I came home and thought it through biblically. I now know what I will say when I am falsely accused again: "Sir, God has not given you either the power or the right to judge my motives, which, in fact, you have just misjudged. I therefore call on you to repent and seek forgiveness from God and from me."

But James does not tell you to forget all about motives, since you cannot judge another's motives. He makes it clear that since others cannot judge your motives, you must. God lays that responsibility upon you. Others may misunderstand and charge you with sin. What is important, according to James, is not what others think or say, but what you know to be true before God. You must be sure that your motives are right.

You must be sure that, above all else, you are acting principally out of love for another. Other thoughts—thoughts of personal advantage, perhaps—may go through your mind, but you should reject them, and without any self-deceit, go ahead to "do well" knowing all the while that God is aware of what is going on inside of you.

When you know that your motives are in accord with the Bible, you must continue in your course, doing well, regardless of what others may do or say. That is plain because it is James, himself, who writes, "Whoever knows to do good and doesn't, that is sin for him" (James 4:17). Moreover, you should not judge others' thoughts by concluding that "they are probably thinking that I am doing this from the wrong motives." There are many subtle twists to the whole question, as you can see. But they are all straightened out if you simply follow the principles James gives you:

1. Don't judge another's motives.
2. Judge your own motives.
3. Do good regardless of the skepticism of others.

If someone openly accuses you of bad motives, when you know you have been misjudged, you too may have to point out his sin to him, tell him that he has no right or ability to judge your inner reasons, and ask him to repent.

"But what about 1 Thessalonians 5:22: 'Abstain from all appearance of evil'?" you ask. That verse has been wrongly interpreted because of an ambiguous translation in the *King James Version*. It ought to read, "Abstain from every *form* of evil." The verse says nothing about avoiding acts that may easily be misinterpreted because of their appearance. Instead, Paul warns that evil takes many forms—*all* of which are to be avoided. Just because you have successfully abstained from one form doesn't mean that evil will not pop up in another form to tempt you.

The passage in James that we have been studying refers to a very subtle form of evil that he is identifying and against which he wishes to warn you: the failure to recognize that the very same act may proceed from either good or bad motives. Whenever you fail to allow for both possibilities, you bypass Paul's exhortation in 1 Corinthians 13:7 to give others the benefit of the doubt; you condemn another wrongly; and you, yourself, succumb to evil in another form. Because of the frequency of this fault, because of the frequency with which we fail to judge ourselves, and because of the frequency with which we forego doing well because of what others might say or think, James' words are exceedingly important.

It is interesting to note that this form of evil is one into which the Pharisees fell when they evaluated the ministry of Jesus. They accused Him of doing good in order to promote the works of Beelzebub. Because He was frequently in the presence of gluttons and winebibbers, some accused Him of living a similar lifestyle. Because He was often found with notorious sinners and the outcasts of society, because He healed on the Sabbath, and because of other works He performed, they concluded that He was like those He helped and could not be from God (John 9:16).

These outward circumstances to which the Pharisees appealed, do, in most cases, indicate exactly what they suspected. But not always. The Pharisees were guilty of erasing the qualification by making absolute what God does not. They saw no place for the exception to the rule. Because they made no allowance for James' principle that the same behavior may flow from opposite motives, and because they failed to give the benefit of the doubt in love, they entirely missed Jesus' real motive in all of this: to seek and to save that which was lost. And, as a result, they became His bitter enemies, in the end, condemning Him to death. It is true that there were other factors involved in Jesus' death, but this one was right up there in front with the rest, prominent because they failed to recognize what James makes so clear. Failure to heed James' warning today also may have very serious results.

In the Gospel records, it is plain that, despite what the scribes and the Pharisees said or thought, Jesus went right on doing good. And, He explained His motives and rebuked them for their sinful judging. You too, when you know that your motives are pure, must have the courage to follow the Lord's will no matter how many enemies you make. Gossip and outright condemnation are hard to stomach, I'll agree, but you may not discontinue a practice you know to be right because of them. After confronting others about their sin of judging you, if they persist, you may find it necessary to institute the process of church discipline against them.

Is there someone whom you have wrongly judged? Go to him as quickly as possible and seek forgiveness. Have you hesitated to do something you know God wants you to do because of what others may think of you? Explain your motives and go ahead, whether they believe you or not.

## Your Responsibility

So then, *your* responsibility before God is to judge your own motives. Here is what James does: First, he acknowledges that a course of action may look exactly like a sinful one. Then, he encourages you to pursue it, doing well, regardless of others. But he warns, "Be sure your motives are right" or you will commit sin (2:9).

In other words, James leaves the responsibility to determine your motives to you. His approach is like Paul's approach to receiving the Lord's Supper when he writes, "Let a person examine himself" (1 Cor. 11:28). He doesn't say, "Let others (even the elders) examine him." That is because, as we have seen, no one can look into another's heart. So, Paul puts the responsibility to examine one's heart right where it belongs— in the lap of the one who, alone among men, is able to do so.

James seems insistent on the point: it must be done. And he is careful to point out that the Bible must provide the criterion for all self-examination. Sin, he says, is determined, and one is convicted of it, by God's Law (James 2:8-10). That is why James quotes Leviticus 19:18. In such a case, you must ask, "Will I do what I am planning to do out of love for another, or not?" It is not a matter of how you feel or what others think. It is a question of motives, which you alone are competent to judge.

Perhaps you, like many others, determine what is right or wrong according to criteria other than the Bible. You may consider your feelings, you may look at results of actions, you may rely on experience or tradition, and you may reason from circumstances. None of these, or dozens of others like them, are proper standards of evaluation. All extrabiblical criteria will inevitably fall short. You must compare your motives to biblical requirements if you want to know how they measure up. It takes effort to know the Bible well, and it even may take study and instruction in how to apply Scripture to life to use the Bible effectively in evaluating motives. But whatever the cost, you must learn how to do so.

Why will extrabiblical criteria fall short? Because God determined that you may know what is sinful and what is not by means of the Law (see Rom. 7:7-12). He says that disobedience to the Law (the Bible) is sin (James 2:10). When you substitute some other criterion for God's, you buy nothing but trouble for yourself. When God has told us plainly how to determine what sin is, why should you propose another method?

James says that *all* law-breaking is sin. That is because regardless of which one of the corpus of God's laws you break, you break the same code of laws, and the same Lawgiver is offended. To stumble in one is to be guilty of all in the sense that the entire law, viewed as a body of laws which hangs together, has been broken. It is not a matter of how many sins you commit that should be considered, but that if you have any sinful motives (or do any sinful acts) you are a transgressor of God's law. You have assaulted His law, and thereby, assaulted Him. To commit any sin, your heart must be wrong before God. Break one link in the chain and the *chain* is broken, not merely the link.

In his forceful way, James is saying that it is not the nature or the amount of sin you commit that determines whether you are a transgressor. It is the fact that you have disobeyed and dishonored God in any way at all—in favoritism, in a so-called white lie, or whatever—that is significant. In that sense, all sin is alike. Don't grade sins. The law is unified in the One Person who gave it.

In Christ, there is also a law of freedom. You are commanded to speak and act as those who will be judged by the law (v. 12), not as those who will be judged by others. If your sins have been forgiven by the Lord Jesus Christ, you are free to love and obey God in Him. If you are free to do so, you *must* do so—regardless of others' wagging tongues and harsh, mistaken judgments. God will take care of them, and in the long run, you will be vindicated (v. 13).

Don't forget, you too are a wretched lawbreaker; everything good in your life is the product of God's gracious Spirit. You must treat others the same way you wish them to treat you. Judge others with mercy; keep free from prejudice, self-deception, gossip, and all judging of motives. And keep your own motives pure. That is God's important word to you about motives.

# SEVEN

# YOU CAN MASTER DESIRE

Because you live in a desire-indulged, feeling-oriented, experience-centered age, few endeavors should be more important to you than getting a grasp on biblical facts concerning desire. James will get you started well, though there is more to be learned elsewhere in the Scriptures.

James' words on the subject offer a good beginning because in considering the many areas of human life he touches, he takes a hard look at the forces at work within. James points out three main facts about desire:

1. One's own desire is what tempts him to sin.
2. When he gives in to his desire in a way the Bible forbids, he sins.
3. Apart from the basic innate desires all hold in common, each person's desires are individualized.

### Desire

The word translated *desire* in most modern versions is frequently translated *lust* in the *King James Version*. This is unfortunate since like the word *temptation* or *trial*, it is a colorless term that picks up positive or negative connotations from the context in which it appears. Instances where desire is clearly good are found in Luke 22:15, Philippians 1:23, and 1 Thessalonians 2:17. Moreover, the word *lust*, today, almost exclusively refers to sexual desire. The New Testament term is much broader, as you will see. It is true that most New Testament occurrences of the word have to do with the desire to accomplish some evil purpose. Yet, that idea is not so prominent that in a number of places, in order to be sure that the reader does not mistake his intention, the writer supplies such qualifying adjectives as *evil* or *fleshly* (Col. 3:5; 1 Peter 2:11).

Second, the term *desire* is used to refer to any and all cravings of an individual. While these cravings are always *felt* in the body (they could be felt in no other way), they arise from two distinct sources and are of two distinct sorts:

1. *Bodily—innate desires.* These are what we sometimes call "bodily appetites": hunger, sexual craving, etc.

2. *Mind-implanted desires.* These are desires for money, power, etc. The first, bodily-innate desires, come along with the human being as a part of his physical inheritance and all serve wholesome, God-honoring functions when properly aroused and gratified according to the Scriptures. No *such* desire is wrong in itself. It becomes an evil desire only when it is wrongly habituated and gratified—for the wrong purposes, at the wrong time, in the wrong way.

The second sort of desire, mind-implanted desire, is not innate. It is a habituated desire, implanted in the body by each individual and becomes a *bodily craving* that is capable of inducing physical pleasure or displeasure that is felt in the body when it is gratified or frustrated. Implanted desires may become associated and combined with innate desires in various combinations. These implanted desires are not necessarily sinful when acquired biblically, aroused biblically, and gratified biblically. They are called *fleshly* because the mind implants (habituates) them into the bodily members so that they become as powerful as and seemingly as permanent as innate desires (Rom. 6–7). However, implanted desires are not permanent (Col. 3:5); this is an important point. The desire for food or sex cannot be "put to death," but it can be controlled. A love of money or power can be put to death and replaced by another proper desire, also acquired and implanted by rehabituation. When that happens, the desire no longer tempts as it once did. This distinction between innate desires, which must be controlled, and implanted desires, which must be replaced, is basic to James' or any other biblical writer's comments on desire.

## Tempted by Desire

The earlier discussion of temptation showed how James places the responsibility for sin upon the one who sins. He says, "You may blame neither God nor anyone else but only yourself when you sin: 'Each one is tempted by his own desire' " (see James 1:14). An object of desire appears. Either because your sinful appetite has not been satisfied or is not under control, an innate desire is aroused, producing a bodily state perceived as a craving in your body. This craving urges you to take action related to that object that will satisfy your appetite. The same would hold true of a mind-implanted desire which similarly is discerned as a bodily sensation that craves satisfaction or indulgence. So, as James says, it is not the person, object, or the circumstance that tempts you to sin. It is the craving—uncontrolled, wrongly habituated, or both—that does so.

The reason why your desire tempts you is because it is either not under control or it has not been replaced. Beyond observing these important facts, it is not necessary to say much more about desire and temptation here, but better to simply refer to the discussion of temptation in an earlier chapter.

### Giving in to Desire

Sin is a matter of inner assent to wrong desire, James says. It is convincing one's self that the desire ought to be indulged, even if it is not possible or prudent at the moment to indulge it outwardly, by saying, "I shall titillate myself inwardly and enjoy it in my imagination." Some people indulge in murderous hate, imagining all sorts of harmful things happening to their enemies. That is why the parable warns, "Do not rejoice when your enemy falls, and let your heart be glad when he stumbles" (Prov. 24:17, RSV).

It is this sort of thing that Jesus had in view when He spoke about the man who looks on a woman to lust after her in his heart (i.e., in his imagination). Such a man pictures her; he may even picture himself engaging in sexual relations with her—all in his imagination. This can be nearly as stimulating as if actual contact took place. Perhaps, looking that way at this inner (but not unbodily) indulgence in sinful desire makes it clear what Jesus and James were talking about and why inner indulgence of forbidden desire truly is sin. It is indulging and even delighting in what God forbids! The body participates in the inner experience when one "feels" good or bad. The person perceives the desire—the aroused state of his body feels pleasant when he indulges in inner sin. It is not merely a matter of the mind contemplating the possibility, but the mind and body participating in the sin—inwardly.

But we must turn to the third fact James reveals.

### Desires Are Individualized

Remember James' words: "Each one is tempted by his own desires" (1:14). That word *own* is emphatic and in English might best be translated by italicizing it to bring out the force of the original. It is a word that makes a point of itself. It means "his *individual* desires," or, as Vincent puts it, "the peculiar lusts of his own." It is the same word from which the first part of our term "idiosyncrasy" comes. Idiosyncrasies are those personalized habits of an individual that are unique to him alone. James is saying that each of us has desires peculiar to himself that lure him into certain sorts of sin.

All persons possess the same innate desires. It is obviously not in that sense that James speaks of desires as individualized. But even the same innate desires, in different individuals, are under individualized control and have been habituated to respond to different persons, objects, and circumstances in idiosyncratic ways. In that sense, it is quite accurate then to speak even of the innate desires as one's individualized desires. Then, when you add to these all the varieties of mind-implanted, habituated desires that combine with one another to form idiosyncratic desire-clusters, you can see that it is not only correct to speak of individualized desires (as James does) but even of combinations of desires that are unique to each individual. We all sin, but each has his own style of sinning. We are all tempted, but each has his own special temptations.

This point, made by James, is important because it means that each person must study his own desire patterns and become thoroughly acquainted with them in order to get control of them and rehabituate them. No one else can do this for you because, as we saw when considering motives, no one else knows what you are like within. Discussing a somewhat different problem, the writer of Proverbs gets at this fact. "The heart knows its own bitterness, and a stranger does not share its joy" (Prov. 14:10, NASB). Because there are individualized desire patterns to be dealt with, there is individualized work for you to do.

When you have become thoroughly conversant with your

own particular tendencies so that you know what persons or objects, under what circumstances, you have made especially alluring to yourself, and what desires (or clusters of desires) you have or have not yet been able to control or rehabituate, you are ready to master evil, fleshly desire.

## Mastering Sinful Desire

Two things must be done to master sinful desire. Innate desires must be controlled and rehabituated to respond to persons, objects, and circumstances according to the requirements of Scripture. Biblical alternatives, implanted through the process of rehabituation, must replace sinful choices. Until you replace them, they too must be brought under control temporarily through resistance (James 4:7).

While it is true that you can't directly change your feelings by an act of the will, it is also true that you can change what activates those feelings. That is to say, you may not be directly accountable for your emotional state at any given moment, but you *are* accountable always for

1. Your disposition to be tempted by evil, a disposition (or weakness) that

2. you developed by indulging your innate desires inwardly (and outwardly) in forbidden ways (thoughts or acts) and/or

3. by teaching and habituating your body to respond in such a way that it now craves that which it would not innately desire, or in ways it would not desire such things.

Either way, the individual disposition to evil is the product of each person's own past doing. If he is a glutton who finds it difficult to break the habit, that is because he has habituated his body to crave (send out physiological signals, perceived by him as feelings of desire, to the effect that he wants) certain foods, sweets, or food in general. At the sight of food (or some particular food) the body habitually (automatically, unconsciously) sends forth its signals. Moreover, the body may be habituated to desire food under stress situations (or certain kinds of stress situations) and at certain periods during the day, or at certain places in which it regularly indulges itself.

Perhaps you have a food problem. It is only by countering any or all of the factors just mentioned that you may "put off" the old sinful ways of indulgence and replace them with ("put on") the new biblical ways. I have thoroughly discussed the biblical put off/put on dynamic of rehabituation elsewhere, in a book to which I refer you.[1]

Similarly, acquired evil desires (desires for money, power, etc.) can be dealt with only by repentance that leads to the appropriate fruit of rehabituation according to the put off/put on principle that runs through the Bible. In this regard, notice especially Matthew 6:19-20, Ephesians 4:22-26, 28 and Luke 3:10-14.

While working on the replacement of sinful desire patterns through rehabituation, a process that may take as long as six weeks, you must control desire through resistance.

James says that God is against the proud but gives grace (help) to the humble (4:6). He continues: "So, submit to God; but resist the devil and he will flee from you" (v. 7). Here, the context for these words is a discussion of sinful desire and the problems it causes. James' solution: humble, repentant submission to God and resistance to the devil (who by now may be holding a field day in your life).

If you will notice, the problem all along has been a reversal of the way things ought to be: you have submitted to desire and resisted God. You *wanted* what you got, even though afterward you may have regretted wanting it, felt sorry you indulged, and became shamefully repentant for your sin. Yet,

[1]See the pertinent chapters in my book, *The Christian Counselor's Manual* (Grand Rapids: Zondervan Pub. House, 1986).

at the time, you did what you wanted to do. You resisted Him by resisting His Word. On the other hand, you humbly submitted to sinful desire, in a false sort of self-justifying humility that complains, "What can I do about it? I'm helpless." James says the route out of such a situation is to repent (4:8-10) and reverse the process (vv. 6-7). You must humble yourself before God and resist sin and the devil. You must recognize your inability to change strictly on your own and in true humility ask God for the help He has promised to those who have truly humbled themselves in repentance before Him (v. 6). And, in humility, you must reject your thoughts and ways, willingly submitting to His. You must determine to do His will, ask for His assistance, and resist the devil (say "no" to the desire patterns he delights to encourage you to indulge). Only in this way can you temporarily conquer and control your desires while you work on replacing them with biblical desire patterns habituated by the Spirit.

Incidentally, Satan cannot *directly* influence you if you are a believer. In 1 John 5:18, God assures you that Satan cannot "touch" you. He influences believers through unbelievers who are under his control and the sinful activities in which they engage.

James is anxious for you to know about those individualized inner sinful desires that play such a vast role in your life. He wants you to understand what they are and how they function so that you may be able to control and replace them. He does not want you to remain a victim of desires growing out of your past. Rather, he insists that you may—indeed, must—master them.

# EIGHT

# YOU CAN OVERCOME ANGER

Anger is an ever-present problem. A large number of church tensions and splits are the direct result of anger. That is why James says "the wrath of man doesn't achieve the righteousness of God" (1:20). Anger certainly didn't help in the case of Shirley, who divided the women's society over her own personal feud with Margaret—something that should have been settled quickly by them individually. Instead, it dragged out and gradually involved more and more women in the church. It eventually became an issue for the entire fellowship.

Nor did Jane's anger promote God's righteousness. Jane became so angry with her preacher-husband that she threw an apple at him and broke his glasses. Then she grabbed a kitchen knife and chased him around the house.

Bill, a deacon, angrily stormed out of a deacons' meeting, leading to much future unpleasantness in the church. All this was over a policy that he championed but no one else agreed with. The work of God was set back for months, as the congregation was forced to discipline Bill and work through divisive measures that he took in order to get even with those who had opposed his ideas.

In another church an elder named Tom angrily called the preacher a spotted toad and declared that he had been praying the minister would slip up so that he could get him. The effects of this outburst were so devastating that the entire congregation was split.

All of these things make it clear that Christians get angry and need help. James knew this and made an effort to offer such help. As usual, James makes a unique contribution but does not write the last word on the subject. However, his discussion of anger is deeply embedded in a broader discussion of the Word of God and, according to his custom, reaches into the inner aspects of the issue.

## Anger Itself

Of course, not all anger is wrong. Righteous anger is frequently attributed to God Himself (Ps. 7:11). An example of Jesus' anger is recorded in Mark 3:5. And the Christian is warned not to allow righteous anger to become sinful anger by letting the sun go down on his wrath (Eph. 4:26). Every emotion with which God endowed us, including the powerful emotion of anger, is good when rightly aroused and manifested in a biblical way. Thus, the goal is not to eliminate anger—that is impossible to do anyway—but to control both the arousal and the manifestation of the emotion.

There are two basic words for anger in the New Testament, *orge* and *thumos*. One refers to the emotion pent up inside and the other to the emotion let loose. It is the former term that is used here (James 1:20). However, in this place the word may be used generally for all sorts of sinful anger, whether pent up or loosed.

Your anger is wrongly aroused whenever you become angry for the wrong reasons: for example, envy (Gen. 4:3-10), pride

(Prov. 16:18, 29:23), or when someone says something that injures your sense of self-worth. And anger is sinfully expressed (even righteously aroused anger) whenever you blow up (Prov. 29:11, 20) or clam up (Eph. 4:26) instead of using the emotion as a force to drive you to a biblical solution to the problem that has arisen (Eph. 4:29). These are background facts found generally in Scripture concerning anger. But now, let us turn to James' words on the subject.

### Anger's Effects

Among the many harmful effects of anger is the one that James puts his finger on: It does not "work"; it does not produce "God's righteousness." Indeed, Proverbs 29:22 indicates that one of the effects of such anger is to stir up "strife" and the writer observes that "a wrathful man abounds in wrong."

Churches, homes, and personal relationships have all been ruined by anger. Can you remember a friendship that was broken because of anger? Can you remember a testimony that was lost as the result of a Christian's anger? What about hurts among members of your family that took a long time to heal? Have you ever lost the respect of associates at work because in a time of stress you went to pieces? Yes, such anger works the wickedness of the devil, not the righteousness of God. And if you have experienced the evil effects of someone else's anger (or your own), you will surely want to know how to deal with anger.

Here James focuses on the sinful anger of an individual full of petty peeves and hurtful actions. It is that about which God is concerned because so often such smallness harms His work. Perhaps more congregations have been split over anger than over doctrinal differences. Even in many of those cases where doctrine is surely an issue, the strife and division that accompany the difference are the result of anger, bitterness, and resentment.

It is not the effect of anger on the angry person that James has in view. Too often, in our humanistic, man-centered society is the emphasis found in Christian books. No, James is concerned about the righteousness of God. He wants to promote God's righteousness among men to His glory. But anger promotes the wickedness of the devil. A person's anger, then, may have sorry results for the kingdom of God. That is why James raises the issue.

## Anger and the Word

How does James propose to help Christians become *teleios* through overcoming anger? From James 1:18-22, the main thrust is what the Word of God does in the life of a believer.

As James observes, like every other Christian, you received your new birth through the "Word of truth" (1:18). He is not speaking here of the conception of spiritual life (the life the Spirit gives to believers), but of the moment you became a believing member of God's family. That occurred when you believed the word of truth; that is, the word (or message) of truth about your sin and God's Son as a Saviour from it. Regeneration, thought of as conception, goes back to God giving life (Eph. 2:1, 5). This is described by Ezekiel as replacing the heart of stone (which is cold, dead, lifeless, and resistant to the truth of God) with a heart of flesh (which is warm, living, and receptive to His Word). That prior event is not in view here. The figure of birth here points to the mother delivering her child. It is the point at which she actually gives birth. Conception is the work of the Spirit; birth comes about by believing the truth.

James says that these Jewish Christians were a kind of firstfruits of God's newly-made-over race. That is, they were among the first to whom the Gospel was preached, and the first to believe. Christ, absolutely, is the elder brother in the family, of course. As it was preached, the Word of truth became the mother that gave birth. Now James says that her angry children must listen to their mother. Otherwise, they will disgrace her and bring her work to naught.

## Listening to the Word
Since it was the Word (the message of Scripture) that brought you into God's new family, listen to what your mother says about your anger. The same mother who gave you life tells you how to live it. Here is what she urges:

*Be quick to hear.* The Word is preached, it speaks about anger, and it directs one away from all anger that might injure the work of God. It tells you how to rightly use this powerful emotion. But not only should you listen to what the Word says, you should be "quick" to hear her. You must not linger, hesitating, debating, quibbling about her meaning. Your mother speaks plainly about the matter; listen to her and be quick to understand and obey. There is nothing ambiguous about what she says. Grasp her meaning and learn to obey.

Christians often fail to grow and gain the mastery over their tempers because of their disposition. There is little eagerness to hear. But eagerness to listen to one's mother comes from a love for her. Love listens. It grows out of a proper relationship to her. This relationship, in turn, is maintained by obedience. One is eager to learn more of God's Word when he loves it. And he will love it all the more as he obeys it.

## Slow Down
What does the Word say about anger? Two things: (1) *Be slow to speak* (when angry); (2) *Be slow to get angry.* These are the

two great guidelines James lays down for the control of anger. The second has to do with the arousal of anger; the first with how it is expressed. Together, they say the same thing: with reference to anger you must GO SLOW. SLOW DOWN! Our modern expression, which probably grows out of the biblical injunction, is "Count to ten!"

One reason for deferring speech is the likelihood of saying something you may regret. Because anger clouds your judgment and breaks down barriers you normally maintain with care, you may say things as they come into your head. On occasions when you are thinking coolly, you would weigh and reject all such utterances. The wise man is one who, when angry, closes down conversation and is slow to speak.

Moreover, as the Scriptures indicate, there are occasions when your anger is not justified. Having flared up in anger and spoken, before hearing the whole story, which may prove your anger baseless, is not only embarrassing, but may mean that you have spoken unnecessarily hurtful words that cannot be retrieved. As Jane, the preacher's wife, later discovered, her anger had no foundation in fact; she had misunderstood a comment from another woman in the congregation.

In the New Testament there are two words for *rebuke*. One means "to effectively rebuke in such a way that it leads to the conviction of the one rebuked." But the other, used for instance in Luke 17:3, means "to rebuke *tentatively.*" Instead of charging into someone with accusations fired right and left, you must calmly state your case, expressing how it seems that you have been wronged, and wait for an explanation if there is one. How much better for you to have approached another, tentatively, slow to accuse, only to discover the difficulty arose over a misunderstanding, than to have blown up and be sorry for it!

But it is better still to be slow to get angry. Four times in the Book of Proverbs (14:29; 15:18; 16:32; 19:11) the person who is "slow to anger" is commended. In this respect, God's children reflect the character of their Heavenly Father who is "gracious, slow to anger" (Ex. 34:6, rsv). There are two strong admonitions in James: (1) Be quick to hear God's Word and (2) Be slow to become angry or speak in anger.

## How to Obey

The objective last mentioned is not quite so difficult to reach as at first it might seem. And I am speaking to you—even if you are one of those who may have had a history of uncontrolled anger. Even if you find it very difficult to hold your tongue or calm your anger. You say, "You don't know what this temper of mine is like. I regret saying and doing the things I say and do, and I have tried often to overcome the problem, but I fail miserably every time. I have given up hope."

Yes, I can understand your problem. But you must not give up hope. God never commands His children to do anything that He does not give them both the wisdom and the strength to do. There is, therefore, hope in every command of God.

Moreover, you probably are already in better shape than you realize. Consider this: you have *already learned* how to calm your anger and hold your tongue—in a number of contexts. If you can do it in these, you can do it anywhere else; if you only will!

For instance, perhaps you are a mother with preschool children. You allow them to get on your nerves and periodically you blow up and go on the warpath—yelling, banging things around, saying things you really don't mean and, generally, making a fool of yourself before your children. You're always sorry later and determine not to act that way again—but you do!

Consider this scenario. You are in the middle of one of your worst tirades in months. The children are holding their ears, hiding behind chairs, and so on. You are storming about, screaming at them from the top of your lungs, when . . . the telephone rings.

"Hello? Oh, it's you, Mrs. Neighborhood Gossip. No . . . I wasn't doing anything particular. Why certainly I'd like to hear all about it. Mmmmm . . . is that so? Well, who would have ever thought that. . . ."

What have you just done? Right. You controlled your tongue. And you calmed your anger. Why did you do it on the phone and not with the children? Because you knew you couldn't get away with it on the phone. If you had lost your temper there, it would have been all over the neighborhood in minutes. But, and don't miss this, you thought you could get away with it at home. So you learned to control yourself in one situation and you learned not to do so in another. Who should count more? The local gossip or your children? Actually, you put the gossip before your children because you put yourself before both.

The basic problem is not a matter of inability to control yourself, but self-centeredness and poor decision-making about where and when to control yourself and bad habits growing out of both. Obviously, you must repent of your sin, think of your children as you ought, reconsider your values and decision-making and relearn not to lose your temper anywhere. The Bible doesn't allow for uncontrolled anger at any time with anyone, not even—especially—at home.

As we have previously seen, you must replace your poor habit patterns with good ones. God will help you to do so if you ask Him (remember James' teaching on prayer and wisdom). How do you control your anger at work or on the phone? You will do so the same way with your children. Start applying the same practices that proved successful elsewhere to those places where you must learn to control yourself.

Ask yourself, "Why don't I blow up with my boss? Instead I

blow up with my wife." The answer is you don't blow up with your boss because you don't want to lose your job. That is very important to you. Well, then, displeasing the Lord and wronging your wife must become even more important to you. Get your priorities straight and act accordingly.

The same thing goes for the woman doing a Mt. Vesuvious before her children. She must put pleasing God and concern for her children before concern about what the neighbors think. Then the change will take place.

Self-control is one fruit of the Spirit. In answer to genuine prayer, coupled with obedient effort to follow biblical principles and practices, by the Holy Spirit, God will enable you to overcome your problem of anger. Thousands of Christians have found this true. You can too.

**Welcoming the Word**
There is one other factor mentioned by James that is most important. We have spoken in the last chapter about innate and implanted bodily desires. Here James indicates *how* the Spirit implants those right courses of action, resulting in right patterns of living. He does so by means of His Word which, if you "welcome" (James 1:21) rather than resist, will become "implanted" in you, leading to new thoughts that, continuing with you, will guide you into the new habits, that, in turn, take root within. But the key is your willingness to receive (or welcome) meekly whatever God says. Meekness implies teachableness and submission to God's Word.

So long as you resist God's Word, even by saying such things as, "Oh, I could never overcome my anger," you cannot expect the Spirit to work. The Spirit, whose Word the Scriptures are in a peculiar sense since He inspired them, has determined to work through and by means of the Bible that He produced (2 Tim. 3:15-17), not apart from it. He uses the commands of this Word, welcomed, received with joy as your hope, to remake and remold your life. Don't expect change apart from the Word. Every command of God should encourage you since God commands nothing of His children that obeying His Word, strengthened by His Spirit, they cannot do.

According to James 1:21, you may "put off" those filthy remnants of sin that remain as you meekly put on the Word that is able to save your soul both from sin's penalty and power. Here the sin in view, of course, is sinful anger. The "soul" or "life" is mentioned because anger must be met and defeated in the innermost part of a person. It can be curbed and restrained on the outside, but conquered and replaced only from within. Once more, James is careful to place the emphasis where it belongs—on the transformation of the person from within.

James' terminology, "putting off" and "implanting," equals Paul's "putting off" and "putting on." When God's truth has been implanted so that it takes root in your life, you have begun to live in His new ways. But James says (vv. 22ff), you must be a doer of the Word, not a hearer only. Anger will be overcome when, and only when, the new ways (its biblical alternatives in any given situation) are "put on" by obedient, God-pleasing doing.

Concretely, Paul puts it this way: "Be angry, but don't sin; don't let the sun set on your angry mood" (Eph. 4:26). That means, don't allow anger to turn into resentment by carrying it over into the next day. That is the "put off." But the "put on" (the biblical practice to be implanted in its place) is to deal with every problem right away, before allowing it to grow into bitterness. All that is plain in Paul's words in Ephesians. The new thing seen in James is that the putting off of filth and the evil remnants of the past life and the "implanting" (or putting on) of the new ways, is only possible for those whose inner disposition toward the Word is proper. It is possible only for those who "welcome" the Word in teachable meekness.

The Bible tells you what to do and how. Your inner attitude makes all the difference in receiving this and making it a potent force in remaking your lifestyle. Again, you see that spiritual growth is by no means automatic. It depends on your attitude toward the Bible. If you doubt God, you can expect nothing. If you resist His Word, the result is the same. If you learn all about it but refuse to do what the Word requires, that too will avail nothing. You must be an obedient child anxious to please your mother, eagerly hastening to understand and obey her every command. A right inner attitude, then, is essential for dealing with anger.

# NINE

# YOU CAN BE GENUINE

The *teleios* person not only is in the process of getting it all together, but he is aware of the fact, and that makes him happy. He knows his faith is genuine. He not only hears the Word, but he is doing it and he is "blessed in the doing." As James puts it:

> But whoever looks into the perfect law of freedom and continues to do so, becoming not a hearer who forgets but a doer of deeds, will be made happy in the doing (1:25).

With doubt gone, motives clear, and growth taking place regularly, the complete Christian *sees* the Bible at work molding his life and this strengthens his assurance. Unlike the double-minded person who is unstable in all his ways, the *teleios* Christian is genuine, centered on Christ, and has a self-awareness of the reality in his life. That makes him stable and dependable. He sins, of course. He is not always genuine, but he knows his sin and falsehood and regularly deals with it

God's way.

But there are persons who "swindle" themselves: "Whoever thinks he is religious and doesn't bridle his tongue but swindles his own heart, his religion is worthless" (1:26). Few circumstances are more tragic than those in which a person becomes so deceptive that he not only deceives others but also himself. It is bad enough to deceive others and know it. But to have so rationalized sin as to believe one's own lies is the epitome of deceit.

You have probably met persons like this. Some of them are tiresome bores. From the beginning to the end of a conversation they not only dominate it, but they subject you to a running commentary on their lives and "ministries." Some preachers tend to be this way. To hear them speak, the Lord is working through them more fully than through anyone else. And yet, if you were to investigate what they have accomplished and are accomplishing, you would discover very little. They are all talk. But they have talked such a good game for such a long while, to so many people that, in time, they themselves have come to confuse talk with actual accomplishment.

One man I knew had a habit of saying "Your pastor . . ." this and "Your pastor . . ." that while talking about his "achievements" as the minister of the church. Much of what he was saying, unfortunately, was little more than talk. Members of the congregation soon became tired of hearing him refer more often to himself than to Jesus Christ or anyone else in the church.

Many people have become insensitive to the value of other's time and demand that their preacher spend inordinate amounts of time listening to their woes, no matter how trivial they may be. Such people are so wrapped up in themselves and in what is going on inside of them that they accomplish little for the Lord and yet, because they think and talk about it incessantly, they believe that all of this inner activity is equivalent to real accomplishment. They have a hard time seeing beyond the tip of their own noses.

James refers to this as talkativeness (1:26). The talkative Christian sounds religious and deceives others. But as he keeps it up, it is not long before he deceives himself (as James puts it, "his own heart"). He talks himself into the belief that he is genuine.

At times you will find ingenuine people talking about how they expect to do this or that in the Lord's service, even making plans—that may involve other persons—to do so. They will debate the pros and cons of this or that method of evangelism or edification—but you will rarely, if ever, find them actually out winning the lost or caring for the needy.

It is this sort of thing that concerns James. He wants to show the foolishness of (so-called) faith without works (1:22-27). The foolish hypocrite is like one who, hearing God's Word, perceives (literally, "takes a look at") his natural face in a mirror. He sees that he is sinful; his face is dirty. Then he goes away and immediately forgets what sort of person he is. That is to say, he does nothing about what he sees. The look in the mirror was useless; no change has been effected. He does not repent.

This "forgetting" is deliberate; he doesn't like what he sees. So by walking away from it (avoiding the problem) and turning his attention to something else, he can forget. But the consequence of this is that he dulls his conscience. Doing this again and again, after hearing the Word and reading God's will in the Scriptures, eventually makes it possible for him to convince himself that he is all right after all. Thus, the inner process of deceiving one's self takes place. He builds for himself a very different picture of his life than others have. And especially, a very different picture of his heart (inner person) than God has.

In contrast, James says, the wise Christian looks into God's mirror (the perfect law of freedom) and treats what he discovers honestly and seriously by acting on it. The word here for *look* differs from the one previously used. It means to look at by means of stretching to see better. Picture a person bent over the hood of his car examining some minute detail of a map spread out on it. He "looks" thoughtfully, carefully. He takes time to discover all that God's Word has to say about himself. He wants to know even the worst. Then he takes it to heart and acts upon what he finds. And, he *continues* to do so. That is, he continues to study the Scriptures until he discovers God's solutions to his problems.

When he does this, he will succeed in his endeavor because the Bible is God's "perfect law of freedom." Being perfect (complete: the word is *teleios*) God's Word exposes all sin and provides all that is needed for life and godliness (2 Tim. 3:17; 2 Peter 1:3). And it is in that law he finds the way of freedom from sin and its consequences in Christ.

When he acts according to the will of God expressed in His Word, he is "blessed in the doing" (James 1:25). Happiness and assurance are the by-products of faith that leads to change. Many wait for the right *feeling* before obeying. They want strength, courage, or the feeling of great passion beforehand. But that is not how God designed human nature. The blessing comes in the doing, rarely, if ever, before. One must never hesitate to obey God, waiting for some right feeling. This is an important principle of the inner dynamics of Christian motivation. Motivation must come from a basic, underlying gratitude and fundamental desire to please God, not from some specific feeling preceding each individual act of obedience.

Once begun, however, new feelings often arise and the blessing or joy of obedience will be experienced. But you can never experience this blessing "in the doing," apart from the

obedience from which it flows. Again, people deceive themselves by believing that the emotional froth that they work up
prior to obedience is the presence of the Spirit of God. You
hear them talking about *feeling* the Spirit of God. This is
impossible; the Spirit is invisible and intangible; neither spirit
nor its presence can be felt. The Holy Spirit always works
through His Word. When that Word is obeyed, it produces a
joy in us which we do feel; we are blessed. Moreover, we
know that God is pleased and that brings joy. In *that* way the
Spirit brings blessing (or happiness) to us.

But remember, we are talking about an emotional state that
is part of your normal, bodily functioning. An emotion is a
bodily state in which adrenalin may be pouring through the
body, your stomach may be gorged with blood, your heart may
be beating rapidly. That is what you *feel*; a *feeling* is the way
you perceive and experience the state of your body at any
given moment. It is not the presence of the Spirit, or the Spirit
Himself, that is felt.

And, because the very same emotional (bodily) states can be
induced by other means, it is easy for persons to deceive
themselves.

All of this is very much on James' mind as he writes about
self-deception and false religion. The hypocrite thinks he puts
something over on others. And, for a time he may do so. But,
in the end, he short-changes only himself: God will not accept
what he does, others catch on in time and he ends up "swin-
dling his own heart." He talks a good game but all he does is
outward—a show, a sham. His religion is worthless; it consists
merely of outward conformity to rituals and ceremonies.

Genuine, God-accepted religion always results in works that
please God. These works are of a sort that are "clean and
undefiled" by hypocritical inconsistency. They show up in the
non-ritual aspects of ministry such as caring for orphans and
widows (the helpless and needy who can do nothing in return)

and in keeping one's self unspotted from the world.

Now, let's return to the phrase: "swindles his own heart." That is the tragic consequence of all hypocritical activity. When one is ingenuine, spends his time merely in some sort of outward display of religiosity (usually for the acclaim of others), he swindles himself. The word *swindle* refers to cheating. It means, literally, "to deceive by false reasoning."

How easy it is to deceive yourself if you set out to deceive others. The hypocrite wants others to think better of himself than he is. So he puts on a false front, goes through expected routines, sometimes with great vigor and display. But he often finds himself believing his own lies and deceptions.

He learns so well to use specious reasoning in convincing others that he ends up convincing himself. The actor so loses himself in the character he is creating that he over-identifies with the part. In cheating others he becomes so deft in slanting facts and twisting truth to serve his own purposes that he can no longer distinguish truth from falsehood. The hearer of the Word who fails to become a doer of the Word fools himself (James 1:22) because he thinks he is religious when, in God's sight, he is not; his religion is worthless (v. 26).

James has more to say about faith and works in chapter two, the famous passage frequently discussed by commentators. But as significant as the material in chapter two may be, for our purposes—in learning about the inner life—the content in James 1 that we have been examining is far more important. James wants us to understand the inner dynamic behind faith that is genuine and faith that is not. It is self-deception that lies behind the faith that fails to lead to works.

## The Heart

A word must be said about the "heart" (1:26). Many western Christians today have an unbiblical understanding of that word. For them, *heart* conjures up mental pictures of Valentine's Day with lace doilies, cherry-cheeked cherubs carrying miniature bows and arrows, and the like. To them, *heart* means emotion and feelings. Accordingly, they often distinguish "head knowledge" (rational thinking) from "heart knowledge" (emotion). But that distinction is totally unbiblical. Heart does not mean emotion in the Bible, and the head is never set over against the heart.

Biblical writers set the lips (Matt. 15:8), the mouth (Rom. 10:9-10), and the outward appearance (1 Sam. 16:7) over against the heart. In 1 Peter 3:4 we read of the "hidden person of the heart." The heart is the inner you, the life you live before God and yourself, that no one else can know. It includes the intellectual as well as the emotional (Prov. 12:20, 25; 14:30). It is the source and spring of all our actions, words, and attitudes (Matt. 15:18) and, therefore, is to be guarded with all diligence (Prov. 4:23).

Thus, to deceive the heart is to swindle the person at the core of his being. If you swindle your heart, you do so *genuinely*, just as when you love with the heart your love is genuine. Deceit of the heart is self-deceit that is complete.

The interesting thing about James' words is that the person whose *outward* appearance is religious, but who cannot match this religiosity with an *inner* reality, is the one who swindles himself *inwardly*. Unless you have an inner reality to your faith, at length, you will develop an inner unreality that you will mistake for reality. This is the classic case of the Pharisee who thinks that he is well and needs no physician. He develops a form of godliness without power. Doubtless many persons are trapped in this state. James' words are intended to be a startling warning against falling into the trap. They may also be intended to alert all who purport to be religious to the necessity of examining whether their religion has an inner reality that issues in truly pious works.

If James has rung your bell, and you must confess that—at least to some extent—you have been fooling yourself, the solution, of course, is not more of the same. Hypocritical, self-deceptive fleshly activity will not rectify the situation. What is needed is repentance, followed by Spirit-activated activity ("doing") growing out of an inner commitment to God's truth and an earnest desire to please Him by obeying His Word. When both the inner and the outer realities of your life are in sync with each other because they are in sync with God's Word, and when you both hear and do what pleases Him, then—and then only—can you call yourself a genuine person, who is on the road to becoming *teleios*.

# TEN

# YOU CAN BE A
# PEACEMAKER

"But she baked a cake for her dog's birthday—her *dog's* birthday! She's never baked a cake for mine."

That's what Connie's mother kept repeating during the counseling session. This had been the occasion for a heated argument in the home. Can you imagine it? On the one hand, there were hurt feelings (injured pride)—and on the other, retaliation for restrictions, rules, and punishments long resented. But the cake became the issue.

Fights like that take place all the time—even in Christian homes. Can anything be done to change the situation? James believed so and wrote about it.

Because of the prevalence of conflict, not only in the home, but in the church and elsewhere, it is important for you to understand the nature of conflict, its source, and its remedy. Otherwise, you will find it difficult both to avoid conflict and to extricate yourself from it when you do become embroiled in it.

James locates the source of conflict between Christians in personal desire that is allowed to run unchecked. Since I have already discussed desire in an earlier chapter, our present concern is how desire leads to conflict.

In describing conflict in the church, James speaks of such conflicts as "war." He wrote:

> Where do wars and where do fights among you come from? Isn't it from your pleasures that are warring in your bodily members? You desire something and don't have it. You murder and envy and still can't obtain it. You fight and you war. You don't have because you don't ask! You don't receive when you do ask, since you ask wrongly—to waste it on your pleasures (4:1-3).

James' words are descriptive of what we all too often observe. Connie and her mother were frustrated in their desires. Connie wanted more freedom than her mother allowed and her mother wanted to experience more gratitude than Connie manifested. So they fought—for what they wanted—unsuccessfully. The only one who won was Satan. In these verses James explains why.

His explanation centers on what is going on inside those who are fighting, not on the fighting itself.

Of course, some conflict is not only inevitable, it is necessary. The Christian must do battle with sin both outside and within the church. The hymn *Onward Christian Soldiers* is not inappropriate to the Christian life. But with that sort of conflict James is not concerned. It is conflict between Connie and her mother, and the thousand-and-one other conflicts that take place daily among Christians, that James has in mind. It is that unnecessary conflict that hurts the work of Christ by debilitating the army and enabling the enemy to gain victories.

James begins his discussion by referring to peacemakers: "and the fruit of righteousness is sown in peace" (3:18). He has been comparing two ways of life that he calls two sorts of "wisdom." The world's wisdom leads to strife and contention; God's wisdom leads to peace and harmony. Having spoken about jealousy, rivalry, self-seeking, and bitterness in the *heart*, James declares that wisdom from above produces purity, peace, gentleness, etc. He closes the discussion with verse 18.

The reference to peace and peacemakers reminds James that there is unrest not only in the world, but also in the church. The wisdom of the world is all too prevalent within the church, leading to conflicts and fights. In this regard, the early church was no better than the church today. Too often we look back on New Testament times idealistically. We hear people saying that they want to make their churches "New Testament churches." The fact is, what we have already are New Testament churches. Like ours, those churches were no havens of joy and tranquility. Like ours, their churches were often ripped apart by heresy and strife. And, more often than not, as today, self-seeking strife among Christians was even more serious than the battle with heresy.

James asks the important question: Where do these fights come from? What is their source? And his answer is: "From the pleasures that are warring in your bodily members" (4:1). The problem is within the individual Christian. And, interestingly enough, it is a problem in his body.

James expands this answer by noting that these conflicts have to do with unchecked desire, with failure to pray, and with asking with the wrong goals in mind. I have considered the problems of desire and prayer already, but the phrase "pleasures that are warring in your bodily members" warrants separate treatment. In responding to his own query in this way James, like Paul (Rom. 6–7), locates the problem "in your bodily members" (James 4:1). We must understand what he is talking about if we would reduce unnecessary conflict and become peacemakers in the church.

First, notice how James puts the matter: he speaks of "wars and fights among you." There is no question that dissension and conflict were rife in the early church. These words, along with those in verse 2, are strong terms. They speak about a condition that is virtually out of control. Are you experiencing any such thing in your church? In your home? In your life? If so, you need to pay close attention to James' words.

Literally, James wrote "your pleasures" are "soldiering" or "campaigning," that is, carrying on a war, "in your bodily members." They are fighting for gratification; to get their way. Frequently, outer battles in the church are symptomatic of the inner battles of those persons responsible for the conflict. Ambition, jealousy, self-seeking ways habituated into the lives of Christians by previous indulgence (3:14-16) seek expression and gratification. It is only the new nature, strengthened by the Spirit who dwells within, that is able to withstand these *inner* attacks. Paul spoke of this war within: he too experienced two inner forces struggling for the mastery of his body (Rom. 7:23). His innermost desire as a believer was to serve Christ, with body and soul. But his body, habituated differently, sought to serve itself.

If you are a Christian, you too have experienced this struggle. The battle against the inner forces poised to please Christ is waged by the old attitudes, ways, and thoughts that were habituated into the body by the sinful nature with which you were born. Whenever you (the new you) win a battle within, you become a peacemaker; whenever you lose a battle within, outer war is the result. The reason why you quarrel with others at home or in the church in an unnecessary, sinful way is because you and/or they have lost the battle within.

James speaks about the warfare within you because in order to become a peacemaker rather than a troublemaker, you must change within. You must learn to defeat the pleasures that campaign against your better self.

## Winning the Battle Within

Here is how it works. You are frustrated in your habituated desire to obtain something. You want it, but you don't pray for it—why? Because you have not cultivated the practice of prayer—or prayer that is conditioned by desiring God's will over your own pleasure. Obviously, this is one point at which you can begin to win the victory within: you can begin to pray genuinely, asking God to have His way in the matter.

The next stage of the battle results in fighting to get what you want, or blaming others when you fail to get what you desire. Clearly, this is a second point at which you may forestall outer conflict. Realizing that your desires have been frustrated—for whatever reason—you can ask God to help you handle that problem His way. If the frustration is the result of your own failures, you can repent, seek forgiveness from your Heavenly Father, and do what He expects instead. However, frustration may not be the result of failure to pray or to ask rightly. Frustration may be the result of not wanting what God wants. If this is the case, then, you can ask Him to help you handle the frustration rightly—helping you to want what He wants instead of what you want. So the solution to fighting in the church is to win the war within; then, war will not break out between you and others.

Inner victory takes place through the put off/put on dynamic already described. You must learn to put off your own personal concerns and learn instead to put God's will before your own. This is manifested, as James points out, in the way you pray (see 1 John 5:14). It is a matter of taking Jesus' call to discipleship seriously, taking up your cross daily to crucify and deny (lit., "say no to") self, while following Him (saying "yes" to Him). Also, you must learn to put others before yourself

(Phil. 2:3-4). The new bodily learning comes from the regular, conscious, obedient practice of God's Word (Rom. 6:13, 16, 19).

## A Contemporary Complication

Today, Abraham Maslow's humanistic "need theory" of human personality has permeated the thinking of the church. Under his influence, many of these bodily desires that war in your members are called "needs." The widespread adoption of this theory by Christians, through this unfortunate substitution of the term need for desire has led to even greater difficulty than before. It complicates matters considerably. Now, under the guise of need, desire is justified. And, the extremely unfortunate fact is that the claim is made that one cannot please God or love his neighbor until his own "needs" first have been met. Thus, a supposedly scientific theory has been proposed to justify sinful propensities within. As this view blinds more and more Christians to the truth about their inner lives and their bodies, unwittingly, they will fortify the enemy in their members. Conflict in the church is bound to grow.

You can see the enormous problem that the acceptance of this "need" psychology poses for the Christian: justifying the very desires that James says lead to conflict by calling them "needs" provides a defense for those who are inclined to indulge themselves in sin and confuses those who wish to serve God faithfully. It is important, therefore, to warn of the danger of the need theory and to expose its humanistic underpinnings.[1]

At any rate, the bottom line is this: once more James has

[1]See Jay E. Adams, A Biblical View of Self-Esteem, Self Love and Self-Image. Harvest House; Eugene, OR: 1986, pp. 51ff for a detailed discussion of this need theory.

taken us inside ourselves and shown us that the origin of our problems is ourselves. He says that you must change your habit patterns, those patterns that have been so habituated in the body that it craves their expression, if you would become a peacemaker. Your original sinful nature wrongly habituated your body which, remember, includes your brain ("body" includes everything that is buried in the ground). So your body must be rehabituated by the new nature given in regeneration. The Spirit encourages and enables this to happen as you learn to follow the biblical alternatives to self-indulgence. Rehabituation takes regular, disciplined, conscious effort until in "presenting our bodily members" to Christ for His service (Rom. 6:13, 16, 19) the body becomes rehabituated in the ways of peace. If you will spend the time and exert the effort in fighting the battles within—rather than the outer battles— you will begin to achieve noticeable results on both fronts.

So the divisions within your home or church, along with the quarrels and fights that bring them about, can be curtailed. You do not have to be one of those who precipitate, or even participate in them. Instead, you can be a peacemaker. That will happen when you personally defeat the desires of your bodily members and teach others how to defeat their sinful desires as well.

# ELEVEN

# YOU CAN
# REMAIN FAITHFUL

A major problem in the church today is worldliness. I am not thinking of indulgence in items on someone's legalistic list of "don'ts." Rather worldliness, or its absence, is a matter of orientation—toward the world or toward God. James calls it "friendship," too close a relationship to the world (4:4). Worldliness is finding satisfactions in the world that one ought to find in God. It is, as James also puts it, spiritual adultery (4:4). The worldly Christian is having an affair with the world.

What is this "world" of which he speaks? It is the mass of persons, without Christ, who rely on Satan for their direction and satisfaction in this life (see 1 John 5:19: "the whole world lies in the grip of the evil one"). The world is not a disorderly chaos; the very word for world (*cosmos*) means an organized entity. It is the world system that is under the rule of Satan (John 14:30; 16:11).

It is because worldly Christians are unfaithful to their Husband, that James addresses all such as "adulteresses" (4:4). Christians are married to Christ. To center one's affections on another is spiritual adultery. James may have picked up on

Christ's words about an "evil and adulterous generation" (Matt. 12:39; 16:4) in drawing this all to accurate description. But the figure of God as the Husband of Israel was familiar to Old Testament saints as well (see Isa. 54:5ff; Jer. 3:6-14, 20).

In the context, James is saying that you can't expect God to answer your prayers when you, His wife, are running around with someone else. Frequently, when a counselee complains that God doesn't answer his prayers the best question to ask is, "Are you having an affair with Mr. Cosmos?"

All adultery, including spiritual adultery, as James is careful to observe, is a matter of *choice*. No one *must* commit this sin. He says "whoever *determines* to be a friend of the world thereby sets himself up as an enemy of God" (4:4b). The word *determines* indicates a resolve, a choice on the part of an adulteress. Interestingly, the word *friend* in the verse just quoted can just as readily be translated "lover," as it probably should be here. In classical times, New Testament times, and even in today's times, the word (*philos*) carried the meaning "lover" as well as friend, just as our English word *friend* can be used for both. A sure way to elicit God's enmity, James says, is to choose to have an affair with the world.

If spiritual adultery is a choice, then God will hold you entirely responsible for it. There is never a time when it may be excused. In counseling, people often plead that they couldn't help themselves. But they could. Adultery is an act consisting of many steps, at any one of which the process can be cut short. We have already learned something about this when studying temptation. James is absolutely correct when he points out that you choose to become an adulteress and thereby set yourself up as God's enemy by consorting with His arch rival. Don't blame the enmity on God; James lays it at your doorstep, adulteress. You choose to do it, you willingly participate in it, and you bring the consequences on yourself.

What tempts a Christian to spiritual adultery? Envy (James

4:5). It is envy of others in the world that leads you away from God ("I want what they have. I want to be like them"). The Israelites wanted a king "like the nations" around them. When envy, rather than God's Spirit, motivates you, worldliness is the result (Gal. 5:16-17, 19-21). Worldliness, then, is plainly an inner problem—it is a matter of your attitudes and interests; a question of where you fix your attention. It is never something that you drift into without consciously noticing the drift and agreeing to it.

Consequently, the cure for worldliness likewise is a matter of deliberate choice. James calls worldly Christians to repentance. Repentance is always a deliberate choice in which, after due consideration, you change your mind about your behavior before God. But it has to be genuine; it cannot be a gimmick that you employ from time to time to keep right before God.

James indicates that true repentance involves three things: sorrow for sin against God, confession of that sin, and the humbling of yourself before God. These three acts on the part of the adulteress lead to a rapprochement with God that amounts to a reestablishment of proper relationships. That is what James means when he commands, "Draw near to God and He will draw near to you" (James 4:8). Obviously, spiritual adultery causes a break in your relationship with God that separates Him from you, His guilty spouse. Repentance repairs it.

Many people find it difficult to admit they are wrong. Their pride gets in the way. Humility is essential to true repentance (James 4:10). One woman said, "I decided to come for counseling when my husband confessed he had wronged me and asked for forgiveness. That was the first time that ever happened in the twelve years of our marriage. When I heard him say that, I knew he meant business. It must have been the hardest thing he has ever done in his life!"

Think of it! That was the first time this husband had sought forgiveness of his wife in twelve years of marriage! Do you have trouble confessing your sin to God? Humble yourself; do the embarrassing thing. Don't let pride rob you of the precious relationship God sustains with all those who are faithful. Draw near to God in confession of your worldliness right now.

Others go through the motions of repentance in order to obtain some favor from God. Consider the following:

> A man is unfaithful to his wife. His sin is detected. He is abandoned by many of his former friends in the scandal that ensues. His shame and disgrace are undeniable. He seeks forgiveness and claims to be repentant. How can you discover whether he is sincere or not?

Of course, only God knows if this man is sincere. Often, the man himself will not know whether he is genuine. In such cases, it is always appropriate to ask whether, if he were absolutely sure that he could get away with it the next time, he would do it again. How about you? Would you consort with the world again if you knew you could get away with it before God? If so, your regrets over the painful consequences of being found out were the true motivating factor: you didn't want to go through that again. But, to be genuine, you must be sorry at having offended God Himself. True repentance involves a deep desire to change so as to please God, not change in order to make things more pleasant for yourself. Double-mindedness, the dividing of your loyalties between God and the world, must cease.

## The Change Required
How can you change? Again, by pursuing the two-fold put off/put on biblical method of sanctification in which you turn

*from* sin *to* righteousness. Consider each in regard to this matter (v. 7):

1. Put off: *resist the devil.* If you do, James assures you that he will flee from you. That is, he will cease tempting you (on that occasion) as he did when Christ successfully resisted him. That resistance included, and was only possible because of, the use of appropriate Scripture to counter each temptation. God's Word is powerful in putting off sin.

2. Put on: *submit to God and He will draw near to you.* Then as Husband and wife, you may end the estrangement that spiritual adultery brought about and enjoy proper companionship once again. And, all of this takes place, not by your own strength, worldly believer, but as God provides the "grace" (or "help": v. 6). Returning to the Lord in submission to His will is the same as "following" Christ, just as resisting the devil is the same as "taking up the cross" and "denying self" in the Lord's call to discipleship.

Worldliness is not merely the crude grasping for things or the following of gross practices in which outer indulgence is the key. It is also the "respectable" sin of many Christian intellectuals who consider friendship with the world an ideal. The better they are able to "integrate" their philosophy, sociology, psychology, or educational efforts with those of the world, the more they like it. They like the world's recognition; they do not like to be out of step with others. They want to be with it. Often, like any other adulterous relationship, spiritual adultery begins merely with "dialogue," but ends up by going to bed with Mr. Cosmos. Rather than fear "friendship" with the world (a drift into a love affair with Cosmos), they court it. If, in the next generation, the church will be betrayed into the world's hands, I predict that it will be the intellectuals and the self-styled professionals among Christians who will do it.

I have had occasion to speak of the dangers of bringing Maslow's "need" theory into the church. It is that sort of thing to which I refer. Spiritual adultery happens very often in the area of Christian counseling. But it is by no means confined to that activity. Be on the alert for humanism (the world's philosophy) at every turn. The danger is that the viewpoints of the world are so readily accepted as truth by many with little discernment. John's warning about "listening" to the world, found in 1 John 4:5, is apropos.

But others also can readily imbibe the worldly spirit. When a woman sits down before a pastor and says, "I'm a murderer," as Mildred did, and then goes on to explain how she had followed feminist thinking and aborted her child, you see to what lengths worldliness can infect the church. In time, Mildred's guilt got the better of her; the world's philosophy wore thin. She was a Christian out of fellowship with God—a spiritual adulteress. Because she was a child of God, her "listening" to the world was not definitive; in time, God's Spirit helped her to see through it. But not before great harm had been done. There was something she could do about it, nevertheless: because of the atoning blood of Christ shed on the cross, she could draw near to God in true repentance and experience His family forgiveness. (Judicial forgiveness must be distinguished from Fatherly or family forgiveness. The former occurs once for all upon faith in Christ; the latter occurs again and again throughout this life.)

Probably, few things are more necessary for the modern Christian to learn than the ins and outs of worldliness. It is not merely following a catalog of prescribed practices; worldliness is an orientation away from God and toward the world.

The world, as God created it, was not bad; indeed, God called it "very good." It is the world-as-substitute for God that is the problem. Therefore, repentance involves seeking forgiveness for an idolatrous use of the world. The solution to worldliness is not "otherworldliness," but a proper attitude toward the world and a proper use of it. Christians must not only look for pie in the sky bye and bye when they die—they can start slicing right now! God's goodness and mercy are manifested to them in this life, in this world. They can enjoy the world so long as they use it and enjoy it in the way that God says. "World" as God's creation and "world" as satanic order of things also must be distinguished.

Because envy—an inner problem—is at the core of all worldliness (as James shows us so clearly), it cannot be combated simply by abstaining from the practices listed in a catalog. A person can follow the strictures of any such list to the tee, no matter how stringent it may be, and still be quite worldly in his inner decisions and in his desire to emulate the world. Envy of fame, power, position, or wealth that others are given in return for their allegiance to the evil one, is deep-seated worldliness, and will lead to spiritually adulterous practices of all sorts. It was a worldly Saul about whom the apostle wrote in Philippians 3:3-6. It was the repentant Apostle Paul whose orientation was radically changed who wrote verses 7-8.

The Israelite had to think consciously all day long, about whether what he ate, wore, or did was "clean" or "unclean." Some of the choices he was required to make seem arbitrary. But, when you realize what was happening to him, the problem of arbitrariness disappears. All day long, every day, in each decision, he was forced to consciously choose God's way or some other. The "clean/unclean" decisions were designed to build an antithetical mentality in him. The continuum thinking abroad today, in the church as well as in the world, stems from a mentality that sees life largely in shades of gray. To eliminate antithetical thinking and substitute continuum thinking for it is the world's way of duping the church into compromise.

The injunction to keep yourself "unspotted from the world" (James 1:27), which is of the essence of true religion, is rarely mentioned in Christian circles today. Yet, few things should be repeated more frequently. "Balance" between what God and the world have to offer, "integration" of thought and action, are the order of the day. Your first thought ought to be, "I must be cautious of the world because I could be tempted to have an affair with him, so I must carefully determine where the antithesis lies. I must know what is clean and unclean, distinguishing plainly what is God's way from the world's way, or I shall become spotted by the world."

Instead, today's Christians seem to think that there is little danger of contamination. They think, "My prime task is to see how well I can get along with the world." They consider it their duty to integrate the world's thought with the Bible's as far as possible. The concept of an antithesis (James' way of stating it is a choice between friendship with God or the world) is either totally foreign or of secondary concern.

This inner attitude of mind, in which you choose between friendships and loyalties, is essential to pleasing God. Christian, do you detect traces of envy of the world and worldly people within? Is there little discernible difference between you and the world? Do you know what friendship with the world means in your situation? Is your first thought always, "Is this clean (God's way) or unclean (the world's way) when faced with circumstances, decisions, choices, and the like? If not, you may be deeply involved with the world. If you are having an affair with Mr. Cosmos, there is but one thing to do: repent and draw near to God!

# TWELVE

# YOU CAN PLAN PROVIDENTIALLY

Planning can't be avoided. You plan meetings and speakers, projects and programs all the time. You plan where you will go to school, what you will study, and your future occupation. We all plan. Some people plan well, others poorly. But much planning that is applauded by the world is unacceptable to God. Planning is not merely a matter of following the principles in some management manual. God has something to say about it; His children must know how to plan His way.

God's way of planning involves the attitude of your heart. To plan well, you don't merely sit down and plan away—you must think biblically about what you are doing. Only then can you plan from a perspective and with an attitude that satisfies God. Your hardest work and "best" plans won't please Him unless your relationship to Him is right. And, because planning is so vital a part of life, in order to become the *teleios* person God wants you to be you must learn to plan providentially. You will see what that means shortly.

James sketches a brief scenario: "Come now, you who say, 'Today or tomorrow we'll go to this city or that, where we'll spend a year and trade and make a profit' " (James 4:13). This is the picture of the Jewish merchant planning his business activities. There is nothing especially wrong with that, so far as it goes; we must all plan such things. Why, then, does James find fault? Because what this merchant says does not go far enough. It leaves God out. Not that God should be merely tacked on, but if He is not at the core of all planning, from beginning to end, any planning will not go far enough.

People have asked me whether James' words preclude planning. No, definitely not! That is exactly what he does not do. He knows that we *must* plan; he is concerned for us to plan properly. While warning against arrogant, autonomous attitudes in planning, James sets forth the godly method for planning.

### Planning and the Inner Life

How you make plans tells a lot about yourself. Specifically, and of greatest importance, it tells you much about your relationship to God—how important He is to you in everyday life. If you are largely a "Sunday" Christian whose faith has little to do with the rest of the week, then you will see no place for God in your planning. James has an interesting angle of approach. He does not speak about the biblical legitimacy of the content of the plans that you make; he assumes as much. Obviously, any plans that are not biblical must be rejected out of hand. The real test comes in what you do with the plans once made. The attitude you take toward your plans and the way you treat them is all-important. That's what gives the clearest insight into the vitality of your faith. It's easy enough to put formally correct lines on paper, but to be willing to have them scratched out and scrawled over—well, that's quite a different thing.

James' merchant assumed that he could plan unconditionally. Therefore, in planning his next year's itinerary he acted arrogantly, as though he himself were in control of the future. That, of course, is not so. God alone is in control of the future. When dealing with the future, which is what planning is all about, He expects us to acknowledge that fact. We must consider God's providence (His planning and control of the future) as a factor in planning.

Failing to recognize God's providence as the all-important factor in planning reveals an arrogant attitude. Autonomy in planning foolishly assumes rights and powers that you don't possess. When you plan that way, you put yourself in God's place and claim for yourself powers that belong to Him alone. Surely, you can realize that is sin. You must repent of any such attitude if you have found it in your heart.

"Well, sometimes I just forget about including God." When planning, you forget about God? That is just what I am talking about. He is of such little importance in your everyday life that you don't even count Him in the plans you make, let alone remember to put Him first! Failure to include God in your planning, for whatever reason, is sin. The merchant knew God, but his life was far from *teleios* because he did not put God into the heart of his planning.

For you to begin to take God into your planning, you must always keep four vital considerations in mind:

1. Your life is short (James 4:14).
2. Your life is unpredictable (v. 14).
3. Your life is feeble (v. 14).
4. Your life is entirely in God's hands (v. 15).

**Your Life Is Short**
Planning should cause you to think beyond the parameters of this life. As a Christian you know that you belong to the company of those who will live with the Lord eternally. That has a

lot to do with how you make your plans today. Moreover, because of this fact, your thinking is not confined to the earthly, temporal dimension the way a worldly person's thinking is. What happens to your plans, in the final analysis, is not so important. You are not living for time alone; you are not living for yourself, but for your Saviour. As Jesus pointed out, in contrast to the Christian philosophy of life which puts God and His kingdom first, the pagan's earth-centered philosophy drives him to zealously seek temporal benefits (Matt. 6:32-33). That is because his central focus in life is earthly. In contrast, you seek those things that are above (Col. 3:1). All that you do on earth—including making plans—must be done with that eternal, heavenly focus in view.

People do try to evade James' question—even Christians! Yet, every birthday you celebrate, every funeral you attend, every serious illness you suffer, and every time you sit down to plan is a potential reminder from God that your life is but a vapor, a mist, a puff of smoke (James 4:14). How short it is!

Take out the family snapshot album; look at those old slides or home movies. There's Mom and Dad whose voices are now silent. Just yesterday they spoke, laughed, kissed you. . . . Now they smile at you from a faded photo and with the force of silent lips declare: "Our life was a vapor, a mist—smoke!"

Don't scoff, "Emotionalism!" No, you are the one who is emotional and unrealistic if you think otherwise. You only deceive yourself when you act—or plan—as if you will live indefinitely.

But there is a second consideration to remember when planning.

### Your Life Is Unpredictable
So you are still alive; perhaps you will live for forty or fifty years more. Perhaps not. But the older you get, the shorter

those numbers seem. Think back ten, five, or even one year ago. At that time what did you think you'd be doing now?

Our family has a custom. Every three years Betty, my wife, writes a letter to each of us describing how things are, mentioning our present plans and asking how they worked out over the intervening years. We seal them, put them away for three years, then open and read them. How differently things turn out from what we expect! Indeed, we usually exclaim over those few plans that actually do pan out as we anticipated because they are the exception rather than the rule.

That is why James stresses *conditional, providential* planning. Such planning is *planning with God.* It takes God into consideration when planning, recognizing that His plans may not coincide with our own. It is acknowledging His sovereignty over our lives and one way of telling Him that we do. It is planning that says, "I will do such and such *if God wills.*"

James' "if" (v. 15) is vital; it makes all the difference. You must plan with that in mind. It isn't the "if" of doubt, concern, or fear. Rather, it is the "if" of confident reliance on the benevolent wisdom of a sovereign Father who has promised to work out everything for your good. This is the "if" that removes all others. It is the one that takes worry away and points to the beneficence of an all-powerful God who is conducting your affairs with perfect competence. The person who plans with God rejoices in the assurance that the expert Planner is at work alongside.

Clearly, you must plan. God wants you to. He, Himself, plans. He planned His work, then worked His plan, bringing Christ into the world, just as He predicted. Unlike God, you must learn to plan with a "holy caution" and you must develop enormous flexibility. You must plan according to your best understanding of biblical principles applied to circumstances as you best understand them. But because you are both sinful and limited, and because you do not know specifically what

God's will for you may be, you must always submit your plans to God for His blue-penciling. Then you must expectantly await the Holy Spirit's additions and corrections, all the while anticipating them with excitement! Think of it! The God of creation is helping you plan your future!

Taking God into your plans will keep you from ever thinking your plans are final. The Medes and the Persians, who thought they could set their plans in concrete, were wrong. When you plan providentially—depending on God to providentially handle your plans as He sees fit—God will review what you have done, make His alterations and hand them back to you for your good and the good of His kingdom.

But there is a third consideration.

**Your Life Is Feeble**
Since life is so uncertain and hangs by so slender a thread, since you cannot control its continuation or termination beyond doubt, even for the next minute, it is arrogance and boastful pride (James 4:16) to plan like that Jewish merchant.

Boasting is making unwarranted assertions, claims that you can't make good. If you can't even control the next minute, then unconditional planning is not only nonsensical but sheer arrogance. The only certainties in life are those that have to do with God's faithfulness. Why, then, would you not *want* to bring Him into all your plans?

Let's consider now the fact that your life is entirely in God's hands.

**D.V.**
James writes, "You ought to say, 'If the Lord wills'" when planning. The letters, D.V., found sometimes in the writings of Christians, are an abbreviation for the Latin translation of this

phrase in James: *Deo Volente* ("Lord willing"). All planning must be done in the spirit and attitude represented by those two letters.

"Does that mean that I must go around saying 'If the Lord wills' after every statement I make about the future? Must I write D.V. on my letters?" No, that isn't what James is after. Though it isn't wrong to do both and from time to time advisable to do so in order to help others to think and plan as they should, James' concern is not about some formula. He is concerned about you—the inner you. He wants you to say D.V. in your heart, to yourself, before or whether you ever say it to another. He wants to replace the merchant's self-confidence with a confidence in the providence of God. It is an inner matter—a matter of the heart.

Saying this to yourself is reminding yourself that God is running this world, not you, and He has something to say about your plans.

If you will remember these considerations when laying your plans, you will always plan providentially, telling yourself: "Well, this is the best I can do. Now I'll turn my plans over to God to see what He will do. Surely, He will improve them!" That is the spirit and power of saying "D.V."

Remember in James 4:13-16, God does not oppose careful, biblical planning; rather He tells you how to plan. Only rigid, unbending, self-confident, self-assertive planning that leaves God out is condemned. Plan prayerfully, saying as Jesus did, "Nevertheless, not My will, but Yours be done."

# THIRTEEN

# YOU CAN
# LEARN PATIENCE

"Lord, give me patience, and give it to me now!" That is the legend on a humorous plaque sold in many Christian bookstores. It makes its point. But it tells only half the story of patience.

There are many situations that call for patience. James says, "Wait patiently then, brothers" (5:7). It is not one option among many; it is not a virtue or gift granted to the few. God *commands* all Christians—including you—to "wait patiently." Four times in James 5:7-10 He insists on patient *waiting*. Clearly, God's timetable is not the same as ours. But while patience has a *waiting* side, as the plaque and these verses suggest, it also has an *enduring* side. Patience is waiting for God to work in a difficult situation that causes you suffering. And it is waiting and enduring without complaint (v. 9).

## God Calls You to Patience

James' threat concerning the wicked (5:5), by which he indicated that an end to oppression is coming, leads to the discussion of patiently waiting for that end:

> Wait patiently then, brothers, for the Lord's com-
> ing. Look at how the farmer waits for the valuable
> fruit of the land, waiting patiently for it until after it
> has received the early and late rains. You too must
> wait patiently. Firm up your hearts since the Lord's
> coming has drawn near. Brothers, don't complain
> against one another lest you be judged. See, the
> Judge stands at the door. Brothers, take the proph-
> ets who spoke in the name of the Lord as an exam-
> ple of patient waiting while suffering hardship. Take
> note of the fact that we call "blessed" those who
> endure. You have heard of the endurance of Job,
> and you have seen the final outcome that the Lord
> brought about. The Lord has great compassion and
> pity. But above all, my brothers, don't swear, either
> by heaven or by earth, or with any other oath. In-
> stead, let your yes be yes, and your no be no, lest
> you fall under judgment. Is anyone among you suf-
> fering hardship: Let him pray (James 5:7-13).

There is an attitude and stance that God expects you to
assume during the period when you are awaiting the righting
of wrongs. It is the attitude of prayerful, faithful waiting (v. 13)
without complaint (v. 9), by which you will be able to endure
suffering.

Once again, we see that this is a matter of the inner life:
"firm up your hearts" (v. 8). This all-important exhortation
calls you to inner stability. Unless you are firm within, you will
not endure; with that stability you will be able to handle whatever comes your way. Inner firmness is not hard-heartedness,
indifference, or some species of stoicism. That to which James
refers is true, stalwart, unflinching solidity that comes from a

staunch commitment to God's promises. It is a command to become impervious to pressure; it is a call to abandon all spiritual weaknesses that cause us to fall apart when the waiting is long and the struggle is intense. According to James, outer firmness is an index of inner strength of heart. No one is *teleios* without such firmness. On the other hand, firmness is the result of the *teleios* life.

It's easy to lose patience in times of great trial. That is what James is talking about. Too many Christians today whine and complain over inconveniences, slights, and minor afflictions. What will they do when they must stand firm in persecution or acute physical suffering? Without inner resources to firm you up, you will fall. Is your inner life solid and firm? Can you stand in the evil day (Eph. 6:13) because you are receiving strength within? (2 Cor. 4:16; Eph. 3:16) If not, you must listen carefully to James' words and heed them.

### There Is Hope

God indicates that you can learn patience. James argues much as Paul did in 1 Corinthians:

> No trial has taken hold of you except that which other people have experienced; but God is faithful who will not allow you to be tried beyond what you are able to bear, but rather, will provide together with the trial the way out so that you may be able to endure it (1 Cor. 10:13).

James says, "If others have endured, you can too" (James 5:7-11). Farmers do it all the time (v. 7). They labor for a crop, but they must wait patiently for the harvest. They do not know whether their labors will pay off. In Palestine it took both the early and the late rains to bring in the harvest. The farmer had to wait for both. Like the farmer, James says, "You must wait patiently" (v. 8). After all, impatience did not speed the rains or the growth of the crop.

Next, James turns to the example of the prophets (vv. 10-11). God did not vindicate them immediately from the abuses that were heaped on them by instantly fulfilling their prophecies. While predicting events that kings and priests did not want to hear, they were persecuted for their messages. But they went on serving their Lord, patiently adding line to line. They served with firm hearts.

Note especially, James points out that we call such persons "blessed" or happy (v. 11). The first study in this book, concerning joy in trial, expands that point.

Look at the example of Job (v. 11). Everyone has heard of his patience. Indeed, the phrase "the patience of Job" has become proverbial because of James' reference here to him. Well, says James, if Job could be patient, with all he suffered, so can you. That is James' first argument: If God enabled others to endure all sorts of agonies, He is perfectly able to do the same for you. Therefore, take hope. Don't say "I can't take it." Learn how.

## Two Additional Reasons for Hope

It helps to be reminded of God's grace to others who have endured, doesn't it? If you find it so, then by His Spirit, who uses His Word, He is already beginning to firm up your weak and trembling heart. The Spirit empowers God's children by giving them biblical hope and encouragement (Rom. 15:4, 13). But, now, James offers two more strengthening facts.

First, he says, looking at the long-term view helps: "You have seen the final outcome that the Lord brought about" (James 5:11). That also was part of Paul's argument from 1 Corinthians 10: God will provide a way out so you can endure it (1 Cor. 10:13). God urges you to look at the *outcome*. In the end, God blessed Job far more than He had before his trial. Moreover, in the suffering of persecution, James says, you must remember that Christ will come and right all wrongs (see vv. 7-9). The last vote (God's—the only one that counts) is not in yet. James calls you, along with the saints of all ages, to trust in God's promises. Those promises strengthen and sustain as nothing else can. But if you doubt or forget them, you will lose patience and will be unable to wait or endure.

James also gives you this wonderful, sustaining assurance: you can endure testing and trial if you will only remember God's nature. Your heavenly Father "has great compassion and pity" (v. 11). As Paul says, He is faithful and will not let you suffer more than you are able to endure—provided, of course, you handle suffering *His* way, in His strength. This third strengthening promise, simple in itself, is perhaps the most reassuring of all: God is aware of your long hours of patient waiting and in compassionate care will provide for you.

So brother or sister, in Christ, you *can* be patient! You can learn not to complain or fall apart when waiting. You can be firm enough to wait for God to make His move; if you only will. He has provided examples of others who did, pointed you to the happy rewards of patient waiting, and promised to be compassionate to you. What more could you ask? If, in the day of trouble, you remember, rehearse, and rely upon these three gracious, strengthening assurances, you will find that they will firm up your heart.

## Losing Patience Is Sin

In chapter 5 James mentions one sign of losing patience: swearing (5:12). And he condemns it as sin. The introductory words, "above all," might be misleading until you learn that they are simply a formula that was used to indicate when a letter was drawing to a close and really not a comparative at all (see 1 Peter 4:8).

God does not forbid the proper swearing of an oath (Gen. 31:50; 2 Cor. 1:23; 1 Thes. 2:5), but James speaks of irreverantly calling on God's name in time of distress. Perhaps Peter's denial of Christ—with an oath—is as good an example of this as you could find (Matt. 26:72). Such swearing is wrong, James says, because it makes some speech more reliable than others, whereas all of a Christian's speech should be equally truthful and known by others to be dependable. His yes or no must never be equivocal.

What does this mean? It means that there is no excuse for flying off the handle, or for caving in and taking desperate measures under temptation and pressure. There is no excuse for losing patience when God has so graciously provided strengthening promises to firm up your heart. These promises clarify your thinking about yourself, your trial, and His providential care for you.

Remember, when you don't think right, when you allow contrary thoughts to possess your mind, when you tell yourself *I can't*, you won't endure; you will lose patience and sin. Like Peter, you may even deny your Lord. The complete Christian is complete because, thinking biblically, his inner life is properly ordered. He must be faithful, rightly related to God, and strong within; strengthened by his utter dependence on God's Word. Take James' words to heart—they will firm up your faith!

# FOURTEEN

# YOU CAN HANDLE SICKNESS

James focuses on one rarely mentioned truth concerning sickness: it may be the result of sin.

> Is anyone among you sick? Let him call for the elders of the church and let them pray for him rubbing him with oil in the Name of the Lord, and the believing prayer will deliver the one who is sick, and the Lord will raise him up. And if he has committed sins, he will be forgiven. So confess your sins to one another and pray for one another so that you may be healed. The petition of a righteous person has very powerful effects (James 5:14-16).

## Sickness and Sin

Before going on, it is necessary to point out that not all sickness is due to sin. For some reason or other—perhaps for the same reason that Job's counselors accused him of sinning—people don't seem to hear you when you make this qualification. Much sickness is the upshot of Adam's sin, resulting from the curse on mankind. Yet the cases of Job and the blind man (John 9:3) are sturdy witnesses to the fact that an individual's sickness may in no way be related to his own sin. I would not even claim that *most* sickness is the consequence of individual sin. James is perfectly clear about the fact: note his "if" in verse 15.

However, it is important to note that one way God reproves and disciplines His children is through sickness. According to 1 Corinthians 11:30-32, this punishment comes as heavenly sent discipline when a Christian refuses to judge himself and confess his sin. That also seems to be the case in James 5 when sickness is caused by sin. I say this because, in part, the remedy James prescribes is confession. Presumably, if the sick sinner had already confessed and repented, James would not call on him to do so.

Sick Christians need the ministry of the elders. First, James mentions their role in administering medicine: "Let them pray for him, rubbing him with oil in the name of the Lord" (v. 14). Today, that function, in part, has been superceded by the physician. In part, I say, because the elders are still needed— even in connection with the administration of medicine. Oil was to be rubbed on the sick Christian *in prayer*. It was to be administered in Christ's name. The elders consecrate the medicine, trusting not in medicine alone, but in medicine that they ask God to bless. By their prayer, they show that they believe God is active in healing. That approach to healing is very different from pagan faith in medicine as such.

## What About That Oil?
Many think verse 14 refers to some sort of ceremonial anointing. The *King James* translation of the word "anointing" has caused confusion. There is good reason for rejecting the cere-

monial view in favor of the medicinal interpretation. James does not use the word for ceremonial anointing (*chrio*—from which "Christ," the "Anointed One," comes). Rather James used the common word that meant "rub" or "smear." This word, *aleipho*, was used of rubbing down athletes, administering medicine, etc. The Jews used oil as a base into which various medicinal herbs might or might not be mixed, according to the affliction treated. (See Isaiah 1:6 and Luke 10:34 for examples of this medicinal use.) Herod, in his last illness, even took a bath in oil (Josephus, *Wars*, 1:33:5). Hippocrates speaks of oil as a medicine. Galen calls oil "the best of all remedies for paralysis," and the Jerusalem *Talmud* advises: "Mingle wine with oil and rub the sick on sabbath" (Berakoth 3:1).

But the elders were required to fulfill a second task, which, perhaps, was the major reason why they were called rather than simply leaving it to the family to administer medicine in the Lord's name. The elders were to talk with the sick brother or sister about any possible sins that may have led to the sickness. James does not say whether the sin resulted in sickness as its natural consequence (as worry might lead to ulcers) or whether it was the providential judgment of God (1 Cor. 11:29-32). Because there is no such limited construction placed upon the elders' task, presumably it included both. As a matter of fact, in many cases, the two may be identical. The elders are necessary because, if they did not come it is likely that the matter of sin might not be raised and the brother or sister might never get well again.

Today, sadly, elders rarely fulfill their proper functions. They may pray that God will use the medicine, but how often do they raise the matter of sin as a possible cause of illness? Perhaps most do not know better. Others, perhaps, fear doing so. Yet, James thought the inner state of the sick Christian was so important that it was the one matter on which he focused all his attention. This element, properly attended to by elders, makes their visit important, and may be the factor that makes all the difference in the healing of the sick.

Are you an elder? Maybe you would like to ask, "How do I go about raising the issue with a sick person?" Here is one suggestion: Begin by reading James 5:14-16. Then commend the brother or sister for calling you (if he or she did; otherwise, gently remind him of the obligation). Next, suggest that you are about to pray, consecrating the medicine and the ministry of the doctors and nurses in the Lord's name. Then, kindly (but clearly) ask something like this: "Before I pray, is there any sin you know that may have led to this illness, either as a natural result or as a disciplinary act of our Heavenly Father?" If the afflicted person has questions, explain the passage: "James raises the possibility of this and, if it is a factor in your illness, you should repent and confess your sin to any others involved in order to effect reconciliation. We'll set up an appointment for the necessary people to visit you right away if it is the problem. I don't know whether sin is behind your illness, but if it is, God says we should help you deal with it at this time." You might want to put it differently in words more comfortable to you, but these essentials should be mentioned.

If there are questions about verse 16, "confess your sins to one another," make it clear that it is not only to God that sins should be confessed, but also to any other brother or sister who has been wronged. It is not to the elders that the confession is to be made, except incidentally, in order to elicit advice and help from them.


## Prayer
According to the instruction in James 5:14, the primary act the elders perform is praying, not the rubbing with oil. That is because it is "the Lord" who will raise the sick one up (v. 15).

Believing prayer "delivers" him because it brings God into the picture. God uses medicine (at creation He stocked the world with chemicals, medicinal plants, etc., that would promote healing). Yet, it is He who promises to heal. Prayer, then— asking God to heal—is the prime condition, and must always be offered, whether the illness is sin-engendered or not. In either case, it is the Lord who raises the sick.

## Calling the Elders

Why call the elders? In addition to offering prayers and rubbing the sick person with oil, there are other reasons for having elders present. First, it is important to recognize that knowledge of the illness does not always get out to the elders along the grapevine. The sick Christian knows he is sick even if no one else does. So in order to assure contact, the sick person must take the initiative. That doesn't mean the elders cannot call on a person if he does not request their presence. But it does mean the sick person shouldn't expect the elders if he fails to inform them. And surely he has no occasion for complaining if they don't.

But why the elders? Because it is their duty to care for the members of the flock (Heb. 13:17). Part of their duty, like the apostles, is to pray for the members of the flock (Acts 6:4). This is one of those occasions that especially calls for their prayers. But particularly, it is their duty, as those that must give an account for each member of the flock, to raise the matter of possible sin. If there is sin, the elders would be best prepared to advise the sick believer and arrange the necessary reconciliation interviews.

Today, Christians too often assume that sickness is always a matter of natural, organic causes and cures. Yet it is apparent that internal factors, such as one's relationship to God or other Christians, may indeed be an important factor. And, whether there is sin to confess or not, believing prayer is requisite to obtaining the Lord's healing.

So, as before, James has looked beneath the surface in discussing sickness and its causes. When you are taken ill, in addition to what medical personnel may say, don't forget James' deeper analysis. Don't create problems for others or for yourself, finding sin where there is none, as Job's counselors did. But, on the other hand, don't view sickness so superficially that you miss any inner element involved in it. Thank the elders for raising the matter of possible sin. And, if they don't, mention the fact to them in a way that will encourage them to perform this duty more conscientiously.

# FIFTEEN

# WHAT ALL THIS MEANS TO YOU

Plainly James intended his emphasis on the inner dynamics of Christian living to have an impact on you. In this concluding chapter, therefore, let me point out the implications of our studies for your life.

## God Wants Your Heart

It may seem strange to you after studying this book, that James has been thought to teach the transformation of the individual by outer conformity to God's Law. It was something like that which led Martin Luther to question its place in the canon, calling it "a right strawy epistle." But, as you have seen, James' deepest concern is exactly the opposite.

In producing the "complete" Christian, one whose works give evidence of sincere, saving faith, James goes to lengths to show it is only when the whole person functions God's way that this is possible. Outer actions must be in sync with and stem from inner realities. As James' teaching echoes and amplifies the Sermon on the Mount throughout, so too in this important matter of inwardness James has caught the underlying theme of Jesus' teaching. The Sermon on the Mount is a plea for righteousness that exceeds that of the scribes and Pharisees. Inward righteousness does not mean exceeding in quantity, but in power and in reality. Those two qualities are inner qualities. What Jesus affirmed throughout Matthew 5–7, James reaffirms in his book.

The focus on heart commitment is clear not only in explicit statements, but also in James' great concern to explicate the functioning of the inner life. He never seems to get away from it for very long.

Luther, missing the point, failed to see that Paul contrasted spurious works (in Hebrews they are called "dead works"), amounting to mere outward conformity to God's revealed will with genuine faith, while James contrasted dead faith with living works that flow from an inner spiritual reality. Getting the inner and the outer in sync is the concern of both writers.


## Completeness Is the Goal

James' emphasis on inward vitality is not for its own sake. True, living reality leads to wholeness that honors God. Vital inner life is the means to completeness.

Too much has been said about the fact that once saved we are still sinners. Yes, it is true that we are. But it is equally true that as redeemed sinners we have a much greater potential for righteous living than you may recognize. The overemphasis on continuing sinfulness has clouded this fact, led to discouragement, issued in low-level living, and tempted many Christians to give up.

James wants us to realize our full potential in Christ. He sets the goal of completeness before us, not as an abstract fantasy, but as a goal fully attainable in Him. James wants us to be well-rounded Christian men and women who in every area

of life are progressing. He wants us to be growing in completeness every day, with equal growth in each aspect of life. Un-
ashamedly, he calls us to a doubt-free life of power in which
prayer prevails, rejoicing in trials is a certainty, and self-deception is eliminated.

## What Will You Do?

James' examples—the examples of an effective preacher—are
impressive; they penetrate and convict. He talks about those
who take a look at the mirror of God's Word, but go away and
forget what they've seen. Likewise, he describes those whose
lives are transformed by that Word because they heeded it.
Which will you be?

You have been looking into God's message revealed through
the Apostle James. You know what you lack in completeness
and what to do about that. You have been warned of dangers,
hindrances, and false steps that you might take. You have
learned about the put off/put on dynamic of change. You have
been told what to do to implement God's commands. One
question remains: Will you?

The choice is yours. No one can make it for you. If you do
not determine to take the first step toward a more complete
life right now, chances are you will not do so later on.

How can you begin? What should you do first?

1. Go back over what you have read, skimming each chapter, or simply reading the table of contents if that is sufficient.

2. From this review, in the space provided on the following
pages, make a note of the areas in which you recognize your
own needs.

3. Then, pray about each (be sure to consult the chapter on
prayer, if necessary), asking God to give you wisdom. Pray also
for opportunity and strength to do all God commands to become more complete.

4. List specifically what must be done.

5. Next to each item on the list, schedule when you begin to do what you must do, where you will do it, exactly how you will go about doing it, and what the results are.

6. Put your plan into practice; all else is futility unless you do.

## AREAS OF INCOMPLETENESS

*Areas*

*Check
here when you have
prayed about it*

1

2

3

4

5

6

7

8

9

10

11

12

13

14

## WHAT TO DO

## *WHAT TO DO ABOUT* _____

Spell out your problem specifically.


Spell out specific things God wants you to do.


State how, specifically.



Where?



When?



How did it turn out?